Liyuanxi – Chinese 'Pear Garden Theatre'

FORMS OF DRAMA

Forms of Drama meets the need for accessible, mid-length volumes that offer undergraduate readers authoritative guides to the distinct forms of global drama. From classical Greek tragedy to Chinese Pear Garden theatre, cabaret to *kathakali*, the series equips readers with models and methodologies for analysing a wide range of performance practices and engaging with these as 'craft'.

SERIES EDITOR: SIMON SHEPHERD

Cabaret
978-1-3501-4025-7
William Grange

Classical Greek Tragedy
978-1-3501-4456-9
Judith Fletcher

The Commedia dell'Arte
978-1-3501-4418-7
Domenico Pietropaolo

Pageant
978-1-3501-4451-4
Joan FitzPatrick Dean

Romantic Comedy
978-1-3501-8337-7
Trevor R. Griffiths

Satire
978-1-3501-4007-3
Joel Schechter

Tragicomedy
978-1-3501-4430-9
Brean Hammond

Forthcoming
Badhai: Hijra-Khwaja Sira-Trans *Performance across Borders in South Asia*
978-1-3501-7453-5
Adnan Hossain, Claire Pamment and Jeff Roy

Liyuanxi – Chinese 'Pear Garden Theatre'

Josh Stenberg

methuen | drama

LONDON • NEW YORK • OXFORD • NEW DELHI • SYDNEY

METHUEN DRAMA
Bloomsbury Publishing Plc
50 Bedford Square, London, WC1B 3DP, UK
1385 Broadway, New York, NY 10018, USA
29 Earlsfort Terrace, Dublin 2, Ireland

BLOOMSBURY, METHUEN DRAMA and the Methuen Drama logo are
trademarks of Bloomsbury Publishing Plc

First published in Great Britain 2023
This paperback edition published 2024

Copyright © Josh Stenberg, 2023

Josh Stenberg has asserted his right under the Copyright, Designs and
Patents Act, 1988, to be identified as author of this work.

Series preface © Simon Shepherd

For legal purposes the Acknowledgements on pp. xvi–xvii constitute an
extension of this copyright page.

Series design by Charlotte Daniels

All rights reserved. No part of this publication may be reproduced or
transmitted in any form or by any means, electronic or mechanical,
including photocopying, recording, or any information storage or retrieval
system, without prior permission in writing from the publishers.

Bloomsbury Publishing Plc does not have any control over, or responsibility for,
any third-party websites referred to or in this book. All internet addresses given in
this book were correct at the time of going to press. The author and publisher
regret any inconvenience caused if addresses have changed or sites have
ceased to exist, but can accept no responsibility for any such changes.

A catalogue record for this book is available from the British Library.

Library of Congress Cataloging-in-Publication Data
Names: Stenberg, Josh, author.
Title: Liyuanxi - Chinese 'Pear Garden Theatre' / Josh Stenberg.
Other titles: Chinese 'Pear Garden Theatre'
Description: London ; New York : Bloomsbury Academic, 2023. | Series: Forms of
drama | Includes bibliographical references and index.
Identifiers: LCCN 2022016684 (print) | LCCN 2022016685 (ebook) |
ISBN 9781350157392 (hardback) | ISBN 9781350157385 (paperback) |
ISBN 9781350157415 (ebook) | ISBN 9781350157408 (epub)
Subjects: LCSH: Operas, Chinese–China–Fujian Sheng–History and criticism. |
Theater–China–Fujian Sheng–History.
Classification: LCC ML1751.C57 F85 2023 (print) | LCC ML1751.C57 (ebook) |
DDC 782.1095124/5–dc23/eng/202208051
LC record available at https://lccn.loc.gov/2022016684
LC ebook record available at https://lccn.loc.gov/2022016685

ISBN:	HB:	978-1-3501-5739-2
	PB:	978-1-3501-5738-5
	ePDF:	978-1-3501-5741-5
	eBook:	978-1-3501-5740-8

Series: Forms of Drama

Typeset by Integra Software Services Pvt. Ltd.

To find out more about our authors and books visit www.bloomsbury.com
and sign up for our newsletters.

CONTENTS

List of figures vii
Series preface ix
Preface xiv
Acknowledgements xvi

Introduction: *Liyuanxi* in the family of
  Chinese theatres 1
Quanzhou and Hokkien culture and identity 5
Origin of the genre name and role of Marshal Tian 11
Three tendencies of *liyuanxi* 14

1 *Liyuanxi* history 16
Early history and textual heritage 16
Liyuanxi in the modern era 24
Liyuanxi and society 39
Diasporic *liyuanxi* 47

2 Performance foundations and style 58
Aesthetics and technique 58
Stage motion 61
Role types 63
Liyuanxi speech, music and prosody 66
Make-up, costumes, stages 70
Watching 'The Great Melancholy' 72

3 Repertoire 76
Overview 76
Traditional romantic play: *Chen San and Wuniang* 84

CONTENTS

Traditional ghost play: *Zhu Wen and the Lucky Coins* 88
Traditional humorous play: *Zhu Maichen* 90
Contemporary tragic play: *The Chaste Woman's Lament* 95
Contemporary humorous play: *Scholar Dong and Madam Li* 99
Revising for gender: *The Imperial Stele* 102

Conclusions 107

Notes 110
Bibliography 145
Index 162

FIGURES

1.1 He Shumin, the singer of one of the first *liyuanxi* recordings and a pioneer female performer. Image by courtesy of the FPLET 26

1.2 Xu Maocai 許茂才 (1903–80), a *dan* from a *xianan* troupe, participated in training the first PRC generation of performers. Image by courtesy of the FPLET 27

1.3 The clown Yao Suqin 姚蘇秦 (1919–92) was sold into a troupe at age nine and as an adult transitioned to 'greater Pear Garden' repertoires. After 1953, he taught all three *liyuanxi* tendencies. He appears here in the role of Yitong in *Yitong Settles the Rice-Cake Accounts* (*Yitong suan guo zhang* 義童算粿賬). Image by courtesy of the FPLET 28

1.4 Wang Renjie. Image by courtesy of the FPLET 36

2.1 Li Hong 李紅 and Lin Qiuhan 林秋韓 demonstrate the 'heart-press gait'. Image by courtesy of the FPLET 63

2.2 Student actors in the seven role types in the fifth year of theatre school, c. 2002. From left to right: sheng, wai, dan, jing, tie, mo, chou. Image by courtesy of the FPLET 64

2.3 You Yubin 尤毓彬, a member of the troupe since 1996, and chief drummer since 2006. Image by courtesy of the FPLET 68

3.1 1954 Performance of *Chen San and Wuniang*, with Su Wushui 蘇烏水 (c. 1931–2019) in the role of Wuniang and Su Ou 蘇鷗 (b. 1934) in the role of her maid, Yichun 益春. Both transitioned from being child actors before the revolution to becoming members of the state theatre in the early 1950s. Image by courtesy of the FPLET 85

3.2 Programme of *The Chaste Woman's Lament* for 1988 performances in Beijing, designed by Wang Renjie's good friend, the Quanzhou artist and calligrapher Lin Jianpu 林劍僕. Image by courtesy of the FPLET 96

3.3 Scholar Dong (Gong Wanli 龔萬里) and Madam Li (Zeng Jingping) celebrate the triumph of love at the conclusion of *Scholar Dong and Madam Li*. Image by courtesy of the FPLET 99

SERIES PREFACE

The scope of this series is scripted aesthetic activity that works by means of personation.

Scripting is done in a wide variety of ways. It may, most obviously, be the more or less detailed written text familiar in the stage play of the western tradition, which not only provides lines to be spoken but directions for speaking them. Or it may be a set of instructions, a structure or scenario, on the basis of which performers improvise, drawing, as they do so, on an already learnt repertoire of routines and responses. Or there may be nothing written, just sets of rules, arrangements and even speeches orally handed down over time. The effectiveness of such unwritten scripting can be seen in the behaviour of audiences, who, without reading a script, have learnt how to conduct themselves appropriately at the different activities they attend. For one of the key things that unwritten script specifies and assumes is the relationship between the various groups of participants, including the separation, or not, between doers and watchers.

What is scripted is specifically an aesthetic activity. That specification distinguishes drama from non-aesthetic activity using personation. Following the work of Erving Goffman in the mid-1950s, especially his book *The Presentation of Self in Everyday Life*, the social sciences have made us richly aware of the various ways in which human interactions are performed. Going shopping, for example, is a performance in that we present a version of ourselves in each encounter we make. We may indeed have changed our clothes before setting out. This, though, is a social performance.

The distinction between social performance and aesthetic activity is not clear-cut. The two sorts of practice overlap

SERIES PREFACE

and mingle with one another. An activity may be more or less aesthetic, but the crucial distinguishing feature is the status of the aesthetic element. Going shopping may contain an aesthetic element – decisions about clothes and shoes to wear – but its purpose is not deliberately to make an aesthetic activity or to mark itself as different from everyday social life. The aesthetic element is not regarded as a general requirement. By contrast a courtroom trial may be seen as a social performance, in that it has an important social function, but it is at the same time extensively scripted, with prepared speeches, costumes and choreography. This scripted aesthetic element assists the social function in that it conveys a sense of more than everyday importance and authority to proceedings which can have life-changing impact. Unlike the activity of going shopping the aesthetic element here is not optional. Derived from tradition it is a required component that gives the specific identity to the activity.

It is defined as an activity in that, in a way different from a painting of Rembrandt's mother or a statue of Ramesses II, something is made to happen over time. And, unlike a symphony concert or firework display, that activity works by means of personation. Such personation may be done by imitating and interpreting – 'inhabiting' – other human beings, fictional or historical, and it may use the bodies of human performers or puppets. But it may also be done by a performer who produces a version of their own self, such as a stand-up comedian or court official on duty, or by a performer who, through doing the event, acquires a self with special status as with the *hijras* securing their sacredness by doing the ritual practice of *badhai*.

Some people prefer to call many of these sorts of scripted aesthetic events not drama but cultural performance. But there are problems with this. First, such labelling tends to keep in place an old-fashioned idea of Western scholarship that drama, with its origins in ancient Greece, is a specifically European 'high' art. Everything outside it is then potentially, and damagingly, consigned to a domain which may be neither

SERIES PREFACE

'art' nor 'high'. Instead the European stage play and its like can best be regarded as a subset of the general category, distinct from the rest in that two groups of people come together in order specifically to present and watch a story being acted out by imitating other persons and settings. Thus the performance of a stage play in this tradition consists of two levels of activity using personation: the interaction of audience and performers and the interaction between characters in a fictional story.

The second problem with the category of cultural performance is that it downplays the significance and persistence of script, in all its varieties. With its roots in the traditional behaviours and beliefs of a society, script gives specific instructions for the form – the materials, the structure and sequence – of the aesthetic activity, the drama. So too, as we have noted, script defines the relationships between those who are present in different capacities at the event.

It is only by attending to what is scripted, to the form of the drama, that we can best analyse its functions and pleasures. At its most simple, analysis of form enables us to distinguish between different sorts of aesthetic activity. The masks used in *kathakali* look different from those used in commedia dell'arte. They are made of different materials, designs and colours. The roots of those differences lie in their separate cultural traditions and systems of living. For similar reasons the puppets of *karagoz* and *wayang* differ. But perhaps more importantly the attention to form provides a basis for exploring the operation and effects of a particular work. Those who regularly participate in and watch drama, of whatever sort, learn to recognize and remember the forms of what they see and hear. When one drama has family resemblances to another, in its organization and use of materials, structure and sequences, those who attend it develop expectations as to how it will – or indeed should – operate. It then becomes possible to specify how a particular work subverts, challenges or enhances these expectations.

Expectation doesn't only govern response to individual works, however. It can shape, indeed has shaped, assumptions

SERIES PREFACE

about which dramas are worth studying. It is well established that Asia has ancient and rich dramatic traditions, from the Indian subcontinent to Japan, as does Europe, and these are studied with enthusiasm. But there is much less widespread activity, at least in Western universities, in relation to the traditions of, say, Africa, Latin America and the Middle East. Secondly, even within the recognized traditions, there are assumptions that some dramas are more 'artistic', or indeed more 'serious', 'higher' even, than others. Thus it may be assumed that *noh* or classical tragedy will require the sort of close attention to craft which is not necessary for mumming or *badhai*.

Both sets of assumptions here keep in place a system which allocates value. This series aims to counteract a discriminatory value system by ranging as widely as possible across world practices and by giving the same sort of attention to all the forms it features. Thus book-length studies of forms such as *al-halqa*, *hana keaka* and *ta'zieh* will appear in English for perhaps the first time. Those studies, just like those of *kathakali*, tragicomedy and the rest, will adopt the same basic approach. That approach consists of an historical overview of the development of a form combined with, indeed anchored in, detailed analysis of examples and case studies. One of the benefits of properly detailed analysis is that it can reveal the construction which gives a work the appearance of being serious, artistic, and indeed 'high'.

What does that work of construction is script. This series is grounded in the idea that all forms of drama have script of some kind and that an understanding of drama, of any sort, has to include analysis of that script. In taking this approach, books in this series again challenge an assumption that has in recent times governed the study of drama. Deriving from the supposed, but artificial, distinction between cultural performance and drama, many accounts of cultural performance ignore its scriptedness and assume that the proper way of studying it is simply to describe how its practitioners behave and what they make. This is useful enough, but to leave

SERIES PREFACE

it at that is to produce something that looks like a form of lesser anthropology. The description of behaviours is only the first step in that it establishes what the script is. The next step is to analyse how the script and form work and how they create effect.

But it goes further than this. The close-up analyses of materials, structures and sequences – of scripted forms – show how they emerge from and connect deeply back into the modes of life and belief to which they are necessary. They tell us in short why, in any culture, the drama needs to be done. Thus by adopting the extended model of drama, and by approaching all dramas in the same way, the books in this series aim to tell us why, in all societies, the activities of scripted aesthetic personation – dramas – keep happening, and need to keep happening.

I am grateful, as always, to Mick Wallis for helping me to think through these issues. Any clumsiness or stupidity is entirely my own.

Simon Shepherd

PREFACE

From 2005 to 2007, I worked for one of China's most prominent and prestigious *xiqu* ('Chinese opera') companies, the provincial *kunqu* 崑曲 theatre in Nanjing. *Kunqu* makes a claim to being China's classical theatre and recognition in 2001 as a UNESCO Masterpiece of Oral and Intangible Heritage of Humanity meant these were heady times for that genre. My spell of work there had given me close connections to theatre circles in the People's Republic of China (PRC), especially the various genres of *xiqu*. But for me there seemed no avenue for a full-fledged career in the field, and so in 2007–9 I turned what I had learned about stage repertoire into a master's thesis about *kunqu*.

Then, not knowing quite what to do with myself, I returned to China in 2010. There I worked for six months in the mysterious-sounding role of 'Protocol Officer' at the Canada Pavilion of the Shanghai International Expo, which mostly shook out to sanctimony in three languages, and ensuring that at the end of their tour ambassadors and deputy ministers received the proper grade of ice wine. Naturally, compulsively, I went to theatre while I worked in Shanghai, keeping my ear to the ground when it came to interesting theatre, including not only *kunqu* but any of the other several genres resident in Shanghai or visiting on tour. When some fellow *kunqu* zealots from my Nanjing days rode the train down to Shanghai for a sceptical gander round the Expo, they invited me – after sweltering in pavilion queues all day – to a series of performances showcasing seldom seen and historically important genres.

This mini-festival, held in Shanghai's vintage Tianchan Yifu theatre and organized by the Shanghai Kunju Theatre over four nights, was thematically tied together by the idea of four 'ancient' theatres: *kunqu, chuanju* 川劇 (Sichuan opera), *Shangdang bangzi* 上黨梆子 (a clapper opera from Shanxi) and *liyuanxi* 梨園戲 (the 'Pear Garden theatre', the subject of this book). Each night, a different genre offered scenes from their traditional repertoire.

Each genre of this mini-festival was fascinating, but I clearly remember being not only engrossed and impressed but also startled by the *liyuanxi* performance. It was a genre I had never heard of. The performer was a woman I would later come to know as the troupe director, Zeng Jingping. She performed a long solo scene, 'The Great Melancholy'. She is alone onstage for forty minutes, representing an anxious night and ending with the dawn. The role she plays is that of a young woman who worries and pines, uncertain whether her absent beloved will remain steadfast. From Zeng's very first entry onstage, the performance was mesmerizing – the singing so languorous and lingering, the anguish of nocturnal longing, spurred on by supposition, by dread, all unfounded. The quietness, the solitude of the drama; I was captivated. At the same time, I was phonetically disoriented, unable even to follow the subtitles (as it turns out, since written Hokkien is difficult to decipher for audiences outside the dialect region, the troupe uses Mandarin subtitles for such performances, so the text is not a phonetic match). I turned to the Nanjing friend who had urged me to come and asked 'What language is this in?' and my friend whispered back, 'That's Hokkien. Can't understand a word, right?'

I had at that time never been to southern Fujian, but I have now been perhaps a dozen times. My spoken Hokkien has remained deplorable, but I have learned a little about *liyuanxi* in the intervening decade: touring, visiting, translating and researching, always with the wildly hospitable and incredibly forthcoming members of the Fujian Provincial Liyuan Experimental Theatre (FPLET). They are the authors, custodians and explorers of the art, and I can only hope that this introductory volume provides a brief glimpse, a humble gateway into this old and ever new 'theatre of the Pear Garden'.

ACKNOWLEDGEMENTS

I am deeply indebted to the Fujian Province Liyuanxi Experimental Theatre for the boundless hospitality – intellectual, social, culinary – they have always shown me in Quanzhou. I hope that this book does some justice to their art. Everyone at the troupe – from the inspirational director Zeng Jingping to drivers, accountants, lighting and sound engineers, guards and cleaners – exerted themselves to make my stays easy and productive. The playwrights Wang Renjie, Zhang Jingjing and Xie Zichou were never less than enthusiastic when I had questions about their own works or about the art in general. I must also particularly thank Lin Xiaowei and Chen Huanhuang in their capacities both as troupe administrators and as actors who have assisted with innumerable queries since I first began to work with and in the troupe.

This book was contracted before, but written during, the Covid-19 pandemic. The initial plan had been to write it *in situ*, working with the troupe, watching rehearsals and performances, asking questions or seeking confirmation in the breaks, listening quietly over tea chatter to the matters that are front of mind for actors and accountants, costumers and students, technicians and family members. I had done so on many occasions before, returning the favour in small degree by translating subtitles for international tours or interpreting for foreign visitors and collaborators. That plan of a long, embedded writing process disappeared into the viral solitudes of 2020 and 2021. Sadly, some conversations that would no doubt have much improved this book became impossible after the death of Wang Renjie in May of 2020. It is a credit to the generosity of the troupe that this book could be written at all.

ACKNOWLEDGEMENTS xvii

Thanks go also to Mark Dudgeon, publisher of the Forms of Drama series at Methuen Drama, Simon Shepherd, its editor, and Siyuan Liu, who suggested my contribution. Lara Bateman, Ella Wilson and Megan Jones saw my submission through to completion. My thanks are due to Alvina Lock for research assistance and Emily Dunn for editing work, and to Dharanivel Baskar at Integra Software Services for work on production. Research for the book was kindly supported by the School of Languages and Culture and the China Studies Centre at the University of Sydney. Where bearing on Hokkien theatre in Southeast Asia, the research was supported by the Australian Research Council's Discovery Early Career Research Award. I am grateful to Robin Ruizendaal for sharing his expertise on Hokkien theatre and making helpful suggestions, and to Rachel Stenberg and Guo Chao for proofreading. I gratefully acknowledge the painstaking copy-editing of Gareth Richards and Eryn Tan of Impress Creative and Editorial.

Several journals kindly granted permission for adapted passages from published texts to appear in this introductory book. Debts of gratitude are owed to *Theatre Topics* ('Repertoire Is Technique: Programming Transmission at a *Xiqu* Festival'), *Journal of Chinese Overseas* ('*Xiqu* in the Philippines: From Church Suppression to MegaMall Shows'), *Contemporary Theatre Review* ('Conservative Experiments: Women's Rewritings of *The Imperial Stele Pavilion* in the Twenty-First Century') and *CHINOPERL* ('The Touring Canteen: Notes from the 2014 Tour of the Quanzhou Liyuan Theatre'). Special thanks are due to *Theatre Journal* and my co-author, Jason J.P. Cai, for the use of adapted passages from the article 'Mostly Young Women with Quite Traditional Tastes: Empirical Evidence for National Contemporary Audiences of *Xiqu*' and to *Cambridge Opera Journal* and my co-author, Guo Chao, for the use of my work on 'The Woman with No Escape: Operatic Retellings of the Zhu Maichen Story'.

Introduction

Liyuanxi in the family of Chinese theatres

China in the Ming (1368–1644) and Qing (1644–1911) dynasties was home to a plethora of sung theatrical forms. Collectively, these forms are known now as *xiqu* in Chinese. That term also has currency within Anglophone Asian theatre studies, but outside of specialist conversations, the term 'Chinese opera' is usually found.[1] These theatres were and are performed in an array of Chinese languages and dialects and according to manifold musical systems and movement conventions. They share closely related aesthetic principles, narrative materials and musical foundations, and their internal diversity could feasibly be compared to that of the Euro-American musical stage in its modern range from Monteverdi to *Hamilton*.

Theatre, which before the twentieth century perhaps only in Europe ever dispensed with music, was until recently a practically universal form of entertainment in China and among Chinese communities abroad. Its practice was as regular at the late imperial court as it was in the poorest countryside.[2] Audiences ranged from sophisticated elites at urban ticketed theatres to lonely itinerant merchants at guild hall shows; from pious fairgoers at local temples to mandarins entertaining friends in their private gardens.

From the early twentieth century, contact with Western theatre influenced old genres and produced new ones, altering the technical and aesthetic frameworks of the entire family of arts. A national audience developed as mass media grew and literacy spread, and theatre became big business as well as an important vehicle of political ideas. But in the long term, the status of *xiqu* in a modernizing China, symbolically attached to late imperial or, worse, 'traditional' or 'feudal' China, was destabilized by the demands for wide-ranging cultural reform passionately pressed by younger intellectuals. The introduction of spoken theatre to China in the early twentieth century would ultimately relegate the varied expressions of *xiqu* to a single family of arts that would thereafter be associated with 'tradition'. By the same token, Western theatre and its Chinese derivations permanently acquired the sheen of modernity.

The crisis surrounding the meaning and viability of *xiqu* – originally part of a larger Chinese civilizational anxiety during the transition from imperial rule to the violent cultural, political and economic integration of new Chinese Republic (1911–49) into the wider world – has never really fully subsided. In the People's Republic of China (PRC), established in 1949, the fate of this family of theatres has been intimately linked to the changing political attitude to Chinese tradition in general. This has meant fundamental reversals several times as cultural policy has shifted. In the 1950s, PRC theatre reform sought to 'correct' and standardize *xiqu* performance, while vigorously promoting it abroad as a gem of Chinese tradition and proof that the new regime was elevating rather than suppressing culture. In the Cultural Revolution (1966–76), theatrical tradition was brutally suppressed and actors and playwrights persecuted, even as elements of *xiqu*, most famously the revolutionary operas, became key components of propaganda. In the 1980s, a new influx of Western culture

LIYUANXI IN THE FAMILY OF CHINESE THEATRES   3

again provoked various premature announcements of *xiqu*'s demise. That narrative has been countered in more recent years by strong state support for the idea of classical tradition and the PRC party-state's assertion not only of its custodianship but also of its inheritance of China's cultural tradition. One aspect of these changes has been the revalorization of Chinese theatrical tradition and the consequent stressing of the continuity (rather than the profound modern transformation) of *xiqu*. *Liyuanxi*'s connections to classical southern drama have increasingly been domestically advantageous, given that (faced with Western-derived theatre's claim to represent modernity and universality) the institutions of *xiqu* depend for legitimacy on the claim that they tap into an authentic, and preferably antique, Chinese culture.[3] Today, although hugely disparate in terms of language, movement, history, regional distribution, prestige, literary merit, and musical and prosodic structure, *xiqu* forms could all be described as choreographed song-dramas with roots, some more immediate than others, in the era before Western contact.

Before embarking on the study of the particular genre of *xiqu* that concerns us here, the historical contingency of relevant terms and categories deserves mention. Genres were historically very much in conversation with one another, and later modern ease of travel and political centralization contributed substantially to cross-pollinations. Though genre is today the fundamental unit of performance, academic analysis and governance, it was not a rigorous concept in China before the twentieth century, and in some cases the names now used for genres would not have been recognizable until recently. While variation of theatre performance across region and social class was very great, terminology surrounding particular performance practices varied and shifted, and late imperial officialdom – while concerned about the effect of theatre on morality – showed little concern with minute genre typology. Contemporary theatre history, including this book, often involves tracing the genres that exist today into the late

4 LIYUANXI – CHINESE 'PEAR GARDEN THEATRE'

imperial past, in an act of perhaps necessary anachronism. *Liyuanxi* has ancient roots and repertoire, but its name and specific genre boundaries are recent.

The genre of *xiqu* we are concerned with in this book is performed in the historic Hokkien-speaking city of Quanzhou, on the coast of Fujian, a province of south-eastern China. Its name *liyuanxi* can be translated as 'the theatre of the Pear Garden' or 'Pear Orchard'. There is at present only one troupe in the PRC that performs this genre, though related strands of theatre and especially of orchestral performance continue to be performed throughout the rest of the Hokkien world: other areas of southern Fujian as well as Taiwan and many sites of the Southeast Asian Chinese diaspora. The centralization and standardization of theatre bureaucracy in the early PRC brought the genre to national attention from the 1950s, and since the 1980s has also resulted in several successful foreign trips, both as part of Hokkien diaspora contacts and in recent years due to international theatre festival interest.

Liyuanxi's single troupe, the Fujian Province Liyuanxi Experimental Theatre (FPLET), typifies a successful navigation of the paradox which bedevils contemporary *xiqu:* the marriage of 'tradition' (the basis of its status and survival) and 'contemporary relevance' (the basis of its ongoing, living evolution). Thus, having produced some of the best-known post-Mao *xiqu* scripts and productions, in technical and aesthetic terms the company is also regarded as the most important living stage expression of a distinguished classical theatre tradition. This results in its designation and promotion as 'a living fossil', heir to an art that is 'eight hundred years old'.[4] Slow-paced and mellifluous, with little in the way of martial clamour or acrobatic prowess, it can be seen as a quintessential deep southern counterpart to the more strident and bellicose genres of the north (*jingju* 京劇). As an art form, it is perpetually undergoing a respectful evolution on the basis of a classical tradition, sustained rather than constrained by that tradition's technical, aesthetic, prosodic, musical and narrative materials.

Quanzhou and Hokkien culture and identity

Inhabited by Han Chinese from the third or fourth centuries, Quanzhou became a major port in the late Tang (618–906) and Song (960–1279), rivalling Guangzhou for the South Seas trade, and reaching the heights of its importance with great demographic expansion especially from the ninth to the eleventh centuries.[5] The city features prominently in the history of early transnational maritime trade, a fact underlined by the 1973 discovery of a thirteenth-century ship in the harbour, known as the 'Quanzhou wreck', that has deepened the understanding of the scale of commerce and international connections of local traders.[6] Known to Arabs and Europeans as Cayton or Zaiton, the port was visited by medieval travellers, including Ibn Battuta and Marco Polo. This latter wrote that it was

> frequented by all the ships of India, which bring thither spicery and all other kinds of costly wares. It is the port also that is frequented by all the merchants of Manzi [southern China], for hither is imported the most astonishing quantity of goods and of precious stones and pearls, and from this they are distributed all over Manzi. And I assure you that for one shipload of pepper that goes to Alexandria or elsewhere, destined for Christendom, there come a hundred such, aye and more too, to this haven of Zayton; for it is one of the two greatest havens in the world for commerce.[7]

This maritime cosmopolitanism left traces in the local culture. The city is home to China's oldest mosque, a Manichean temple and Hindu carvings linked to a Tamil diaspora, all of which testify to Quanzhou's history of cultural eclecticism and diverse population. Archaeological evidence shows that Nestorian Christians were in Quanzhou from the Mongol Yuan dynasty (1271–1368), and at least four successive Roman Catholic Italian bishops held the See

6   LIYUANXI – CHINESE 'PEAR GARDEN THEATRE'

of Zaiton in the fourteenth century alongside an Armenian Christian community. The Ispah Rebellion (1357–64), which decimated the city, was a rebellion of local Arabs and Persians at the tail end of the failing Mongol Yuan dynasty, and marks the peak of Muslim power in the region. The failure of the rebellion resulted in the massacre of Muslim populations and the end of foreign arrivals, though Quanzhou would again play an important role in Chinese Islam as the port of departure for the fifteenth-century voyages of the Muslim 'eunuch admiral' Zheng He.[8]

In later centuries the city's fortunes declined, but Quanzhou's international trade and cosmopolitanism sowed the seeds to make Hokkien the first of China's maritime and outward-looking local cultures, and indeed has led some historians to consider the city the northern coast of a 'Southeast Asian Mediterranean'.[9] The culture of the region, known in English variously as Hokkien, Minnan, Hoklo and Southern Fujian, has produced one of the most distinct of Han Chinese (sub-) ethnicities, as well as one of its most transnational networks. From the sixteenth century onward, large-scale Hokkien migration produced communities that established themselves throughout Southeast Asia and in Taiwan. Considerable contact was established with the newly arrived Europeans, especially the Portuguese,[10] and Hokkien became a major component in the hybrid cultures known as Peranakan in Singapore, Penang or Jakarta, and as 'mestizo' in Manila. In some places (Penang, Sumatra, Manila), Hokkien became the Chinese lingua franca. Since theatre was an important part of ritual life as well as a central form of entertainment, Hokkien emigrants brought their theatre with them wherever they went, and living practices of Hokkien-derived arts, including a great deal of puppet theatre, continue to exist throughout the region.[11]

As Quanzhou's harbour silted up, the focus of commerce moved to Xiamen, now about an hour's drive away. However, Quanzhou's historical pre-eminence has made it the enduring classical seat of Hokkien culture, though it now ranks second in the region as a centre of politics, population or education.[12] Today, Quanzhou furnishes a focal local identity and an administrative centre for a large industrial area, including Jinjiang (on the other bank of the Min River) and the surrounding towns of Anxi, Nan'an, Hui'an and Shishi. Several of China's important firms originate in Quanzhou, and many Southeast Asian Chinese trace their lineage there and for that reason have preferred it as a site for manufacturing or business activities.[13] Residents 'take an equal pride in the history of Quanzhou as an ancient trading port and its current status as the flagship of economic development in Fujian Province'.[14] The city has tapped into its transnational history when in recent decades it has represented itself as the origin of the Maritime Silk Road. That connection, a key part of the Belt and Road Initiative, represents China's historic commercial and cultural exchanges across the Indo-Pacific.

Quanzhou's urban population numbers 1.4 million people, while the district it governs (in PRC terms, the 'prefecture-level city') is home to over 8 million. Like other prosperous urban areas of China, years of economic boom have drawn labourers from other parts of the country, especially the poorer neighbouring province of Jiangxi and the Hakka areas of western Fujian. Quanzhou elites and labourers alike have sought opportunities in top-tier cities such as Shanghai, Beijing and Guangzhou. Quanzhou therefore remains an important node – source and destination – for internal and external migration.

Liyuanxi is a theatrical expression of Hokkien culture. Around half of Fujian's 41 million inhabitants are Hokkien, that is, the populations of the southern coast around Quanzhou, Xiamen and Zhangzhou. There are almost as many Hokkien people in Taiwan, where they comprise 70 per cent of Taiwan's population of 23 million, largely the descendants of migrants who arrived between the mid-seventeenth to the mid-twentieth centuries. In both polities, the use of Mandarin for official purposes, at times forcefully imposed, as well as the increased interaction with other Chinese populations, have decreased the prevalence of Hokkien language, especially among young urbanites. Nevertheless, Hokkien remains one of the largest and strongest among Chinese or 'Sinitic' languages and cultures, and many older people in the region (including many *liyuanxi* actors) speak Mandarin haltingly if at all.

Mutually unintelligible with Mandarin, Cantonese or Wu, Hokkien is often on that basis considered a separate language.[15] It shares a closer parentage with neighbouring Teochew, across the Guangdong border, and to a lesser degree with the Hinghwa (Pu-Xian Min) population to the immediate north. These linguistic relations mirror similarities and affinities in cultural practice, including as regards theatre genre.

The migration of Hokkien speakers to Southeast Asia which reached its height in the hundred years before the Second World War was among the largest movements of people in history. The result is that there is still a large community of speakers in cities such as Penang and Melaka (Malaysia), Medan (Indonesia), Manila (the Philippines) and Yangon (Myanmar), although Hokkien communities in other areas (Java, Singapore) have largely lost use of the language. Hokkien is further subdivided into dialects which are themselves not easily mutually intelligible: of these the principal division is between Zhangzhou and Quanzhou. In the history of Hokkien, Quanzhou and Zhangzhou form 'a dual linguistic center, from which all modern varieties are derived'.[16] The result is that the Hokkien of the *liyuanxi* stage is at some distance from the language, for instance, of the Taiwanese Hokkien popular theatre, song and film.

The presence of a Hokkien diaspora and its interest in *liyuanxi* have on several occasions proven beneficial to the genre's practitioners. Before the Second World War, audiences abroad represented an important market for the troupes, and tours offered opportunities for actors to hone their skills and gain experience. Performance invitations from the diaspora offered prestige and foreign exchange in the 1980s in an era before it became common for PRC troupes to tour abroad on their own initiative. In the 1990s, Taiwan tours represented the chance to earn hard currency from a richer economy. Diasporic networks have also had a flipside for the theatre's fortunes: in the 1980s, several troupe members took advantage of revived business links with the diaspora, with some leaving the PRC stage to pursue careers in business and/or the arts in Singapore or Manila.

Although the most 'refined' and literary and therefore the highest status of Hokkien theatre genres, *liyuanxi* is far from alone in representing Quanzhou theatrical heritage, and there has been a constant flow of people and influences between *liyuanxi* and the other genres active in the region. Internationally and domestically, the most famous Quanzhou theatrical traditions are probably the two major puppet practices: the marionettes and the glove puppet theatre known as *budaixi* (in Mandarin) 布袋戲 or *potehi* (in Hokkien).[17] *Potehi* spread especially widely during the late nineteenth and early twentieth centuries, brought by migrants from the Hokkien region to Yangon and Penang, Sumatra and Manila.[18] Practices continue in several regions, and especially in Taiwan – where the puppets, in constantly evolving forms, have become a powerful symbol of the island's identity.

Several other *xiqu* genres belong to the region, all of them owing some portion of their aesthetic and narrative heritage to the older *liyuanxi* genre.[19] *Gaojiaxi* 高甲戲 challenged and largely replaced *liyuanxi* forms in the first decades of the twentieth century, perhaps because it offered more of the military and acrobatic theatre that is largely absent in *liyuanxi*. *Gaojiaxi* is still much performed in southern Fujian, both by amateurs and professional troupes, although in the diaspora and Taiwan it has itself largely been replaced by *gezaixi* 歌仔戲, sometimes known in Fujian as *xiangju* 薌劇.[20] *Gezaixi* is a transnational form of theatre that, although with roots in Hokkien culture, is best known in Taiwan and has (under various names) continued to enjoy popularity in Singapore and Malaysia.[21] The religious theatre *dachengxi* 打城戲, long threatened, now seems on the verge of total disappearance despite sporadic efforts to establish a troupe in Quanzhou.[22]

Liyuanxi has links to all of these genres, including some shared musical systems, scripts and narratives, family lineages and borrowings of movement vocabulary. But of all genres, the closest connection is to that of the best-known traditional

Hokkien music called *nanyin* 南音 (southern music) or *nanguan* 南管 (southern pipes).[23] *Nanyin* shares much repertoire, music and texts with *liyuanxi*. While there is a lively debate about precedence, the balance of evidence suggests that the orchestral and dramatic genres were entwined from the start. Early records of the two genres are inseparably intertwined, but by the early twentieth century, *nanyin* was still being widely sung while *liyuanxi* performance was in rapid decline.

Nanyin, today widely practised in Fujian, Taiwan and the Hokkien diaspora, was in 2009 included on UNESCO's Representative List of the Intangible Cultural Heritage of Humanity, a listing that drew greater attention to all of Quanzhou's musical and theatrical forms. FPLET sometimes incorporates *nanyin* in concert style: for instance when 'The Great Melancholy' (Da men 大悶) from *Chen San Wuniang* 陳三五娘 was performed in Théâtre du Soleil's prestigious Cartoucherie theatre, this forty-minute scene was preceded by a *nanyin* concert to fill out the session.

Musically, tempo is one feature that distinguishes the two musical practices. A direct comparison of the same passage found that theatre forms including *liyuanxi* used 'faster, melodic lines less embellished and instrumentation augmented as compared to *nanyin* singing',[24] indicating a dramatic concern to advance the narrative in contrast to *nanyin*'s more leisurely concert setting. FPLET's larger orchestra also shows the influence of other *xiqu* genres' musical practice. The city's official *nanyin* troupe is often called upon to perform a similar function as representative of traditional culture for events such as the World Hokkien Culture Festival (Shijie Minnan wenhuajie 世界閩南文化節; held in Quanzhou in 2013), Culture City of East Asia (Dongya wenhua zhidu 東亞文化之都; Quanzhou, Yokohama and Gwangju were given this distinction in 2014) or Maritime Silk Road events. It is no accident that the Quanzhou government in 2006 erected theatres for the *nanyin* troupe and the *liyuanxi* side by side.

Locals take pride in their eclectic heritage, unique dialect, folk practices, present prosperity and ancient importance, built heritage, religious practices, diasporic networks, and theatre and performance culture.[25] Part of the longevity of *liyuanxi* has been pride in this uniqueness. The troupe playwright Wang Renjie, always good for a pun, and much interested in the relationship between stage and place, spoke of *liyuanxi* as *gu-gu-gu*: 孤 solitary, 古 ancient and 固 stubborn – solitary because it is distant from the mainstream of *xiqu* culture and performed by a single troupe; ancient because of its connection with some of the earliest extant Chinese theatre texts; and stubborn because it has retained its own traditions in the face of the more visible and showy theatre traditions and despite the whirligig of modern life that is antithetical to all less frantic genres of culture.[26]

Origin of the genre name and role of Marshal Tian

The *liyuanxi* genre's name derives from an older association between 'pear garden' and theatre. This association is based on historical accounts of the Tang emperor Xuanzong 玄宗 (reigned 712–56) founding an ensemble that played in an orchard or garden of that name. The tenth-century *Institutional History of the Tang* (*Tang huiyao* 唐會要) dates the foundation of the Pear Garden troupe in 714, and the *New Book of Tang* (*Xin Tangshu* 新唐書), an eleventh-century history, offers a longer account.[27] Both texts describe a musical ensemble, but evidently the establishment of a troupe of any kind in an imperial pear garden furnished a semi-legendary genealogy for Chinese theatre as well.[28] Up to the present day, the term *liyuan* provides a general and 'standard nomenclature for both actors and the theatre' throughout *xiqu*.[29]

The name is bound up also in the rituals of theatre surrounding its patron deity. Theatre in China is generally thought to have emerged out of religious practices, and all forms of *xiqu* historically had ritual functions. In most situations and periods these functions have predominated over elite or commercial entertainment. Southern Fujian remains an area of conspicuous ritual commitment and, despite the suspicion and sometimes suppression of religion in the PRC, various ritual practices remain associated with *liyuanxi*. The troupe, along with all other southern Fujian performance groups, sends detachments on contract to perform for auspicious purposes, such as the opening of new temples or businesses.

For *liyuanxi*, the central ritual practice is the reverence of Marshal Tian (Tian duyuanshuai 田都元帥), a practice shared with Hokkien puppet theatres as well as with the *puxianxi* 莆仙戲 performers to the north. While the deity has a broader function in Quanzhou society, he has a special relationship to entertainers.[30] Research on veneration of the deity has counted over a thousand shrines built in his honour throughout the Ming and Qing in Fujian and Taiwan, with the earliest record dating from 1379.[31] In life, Marshal Tian's name was Lei Haiqing 雷海青, and in the theatre world he is usually addressed and referred to as Young Lord (*xianggong* 相公). Legends, probably of later origin, name him as a member of the Pear Garden.[32]

A relatively extensive and early account of Lei Haiqing's life appears in the late seventeenth-century novel called *Romances of the Sui and Tang* (*Sui Tang yanyi* 隋唐演義), which is doubtless not the origin of the legend but provides a representative account. According to this story, Lei Haiqing was the *pipa* player in the imperial Pear Garden. After the initial successes of the An Lushan 安祿山 rebellion, when emperor and imperial court had fled the capital, An Lushan summoned the Pear Garden musicians to play for him, but met with a refusal. Instead,

Lei Haiqing forced his way to the front of the hall and swept the musical instruments on the table to the floor, then pointed at [An] Lushan and berated him: 'You rebellious miscreant, you were favoured by the Son of Heaven, but instead you ungratefully turned on him. You should be cut into ten thousand pieces, and still you jabber! I am only

LIYUANXI IN THE FAMILY OF CHINESE THEATRES   13

a humble musician, and yet I know loyalty, so how could I serve a rebellious thief like yourself? Today shall be the day of my self-sacrifice, and after I die my brother Lei Wanchun can fulfil his duties to the state, so there will always be someone to cut down a thief like you!' Lushan stared at him in fury, unable to say a word, except to command men to hack him down.[33]

This legend of the musical martyr was evidently widespread. Nineteenth-century officials noted that there were Lei Haiqing temples everywhere in Quanzhou and that they were much visited.[34] In local accounts, Lei is sometimes recast as a Quanzhou man, and his name is explained by the fact appearing in the sky to some followers after his death, his banner (featuring his surname, Lei 雷) was partly occluded by clouds, so that only the lower part, Tian 田, could be seen.[35] Variants of the legend were once common, but since official publication of a version of it in 1986, the story has been considerably homogenized.[36] The deity's shrine at the FPLET can be visited on the fifth floor. Before important shows or events, offerings are made, ritual prayers are recited and spirit paper is burned. As in temples, papers posted on the wall sometimes note the sum that theatre members have given to a certain festival or to a repair or improvement of the altar. If good luck is requested or bad luck befalls, special sacrifices and prayers are made. Photography is not usually permitted, and only those clear of mind and body may offer their prayers. Rituals once preceded any performance, but at the FPLET these are now reserved for particular occasions (such as premieres) and requests for special intervention.[37]

A number of other ritual practices also have a bearing on stage practice and troupe life. Especially in the countryside performances, certain ritual performances and dances are indicated for occasions such as the inauguration of a temple or a business, or the birthday of a sponsor. For instance, pre-performance rituals are necessary when a stage is to be used for the first time by a particular troupe, the promotion dance (*tiaojiaguan* 跳加官) is performed to bring good fortune in public life, and the ritual song *lo-li-lien* occurs as a refrain in numerous songs in repertoire pieces.

Other practices are intended to ward off supernatural displeasure. Thus, if performing in Quanzhou, an actor playing a ghost must wear a protective spell written on spirit paper in order to avoid supernatural trouble. Propitiation, too, can be achieved through ritual. On one occasion during the FPLET's 2014 European tour, where rain had forced cancellation of a performance in Lyon's Greco-Roman theatre, it was presumed that the cherries that had been offered to the Marshal prior to the performance had been too sour. After cancellation, another ritual was conducted to beg his pardon, and spirit paper (brought along expressly for this purpose) was burnt to appease him. The following performance went off without a hitch.

Three tendencies of *liyuanxi*

In the southern Fujian area, the term 'Pear Garden theatre' was by the late imperial era being applied to local theatre genres. Two troupes of adult theatre, *shanglu* 上路 (literally 'upper circuit') and *xianan* 下南 (literally 'down south') were known as 'greater Pear Garden' theatre (*da liyuan* 大梨園) or 'old theatre' (*laoxi* 老戲). The 'lesser Pear Garden' (*xiao liyuan* 小梨園) repertoire was performed by child actors, all boys until roughly the 1920s. These practices borrowed from one another and shared some repertoire and musical patterns, but the troupes were largely separate until amalgamation under the PRC's new system.

Shanglu repertoire is usually characterized as being principally concerned with traditional virtues – loyalty, filial piety, chastity, righteousness – and is considered to originate in troupes arriving in the region from Zhejiang in the Song and Yuan, although these accounts may be folkloric. The *xianan* repertoire, which is presumed to be more indigenous ('down south' being a reference to Fujian), is a little rougher in both literary and musical terms and features repertoire in a folksier vein, with more straightforward tales of evil punished and virtue rewarded.

The 'lesser Pear Garden' repertoire, performed by children, was focused on the type of romance known as 'talent-and-beauty' (*caizi jiaren* 才子佳人) stories. The creation legend of this practice relates that, after the fall of the southern Song dynasty at the end of the thirteenth century, child actor troupes turned to itinerant performance, since aristocratic patronage in Hangzhou had come to an end. While there were child actors all over China, genres defined as being specifically for children's performance were not common. Another name for Fujian child troupes was *qiziban* 七子班 (seven-children ensemble) – with the seven boy actors each corresponding to a role type. The repertoire, largely romantic and comical, depended on the freshness and agility of children. The stories are relatively light-hearted, and there is a tendency even now to prefer younger actors for this repertoire.[38] Child actors, often orphans or from impoverished families, were contracted from early age and for up to ten years to the head of the itinerant troupe. When the boys' voices broke around the age of thirteen, they were sent back home or transitioned into the 'greater Pear Garden' genres as actors or musicians.

Today, these three tendencies or styles no longer represent separate troupes or institutions but feature substantially as repertoire markers within the troupe, and as such also have consequences for role-type pedagogy. Newly written plays are not sorted according to these terms, although the way they borrow sequences, tropes and narrative patterns may relate them more closely to one tendency than the other. Since 'Pear Garden' was the common element in the loose generic names, when these theatres were amalgamated into a single institution in the early PRC, 'Pear Garden theatre' was eventually chosen as the name of the genre.[39]

1

Liyuanxi history

Early history and textual heritage

The Tang origins of the genre's name are of course no indication of the art form's genesis, though the theatre practice can make plausible claims to being among China's oldest. The assertion typically put forward by the FPLET and sympathetic scholars tends to place the origins of *liyuanxi* at eight hundred years ago, relying on evidence of theatre performance in the Quanzhou region, much of which does not provide conclusive genre information.[1] One effect of such a chronology is to trump other genres, such as *kunqu*'s (equally debatable) six hundred years.[2] The question of when and how the history of *liyuanxi* begins depends on the question of genre definition in *xiqu*, as well as the degree of evidence necessary to assert a reasonable continuity between texts of the past and the stages of the present.

Sources are a thin patchwork. Piet van der Loon concluded in 1992 that the 'history of the stage in [Quanzhou] and [Zhangzhou] is so poorly documented that, even if we include evidence from foreign observers, no coherent account can be presented'.[3] Despite the efforts of scholars in Fujian and Taiwan, as well as those in Japan and the West, the history of this theatre before the twentieth century is likely to remain fragmentary to a high degree, with gaps in the historical documentation being filled by educated guesses relying on brief passages about performance practice and repertoire. Two types of historical text are relevant to sketching a relation between historical theatrical practice and the *liyuanxi* tradition as formalized in the PRC in the 1950s: theatre scripts and vocal scores from the region (and to a lesser extent from the nearby related Chaozhou genres), and historical records from the region (or in the diaspora) that give accounts of theatre performance or practice that might reasonably be supposed to be the antecedents of *liyuanxi*. The paucity and brevity of sources are an issue *liyuanxi* historiography shares with most pre-twentieth-century performance traditions in China, since theatrical activities were considered beneath the notice of local administrators during the late imperial period, and theatre people usually rated only cursory attention.

Liyuanxi and *nanxi*

Most scholars agree that the first China genre that 'can certainly be classified as real and fully developed drama' is *nanxi* 南戲 (literally 'southern drama'), usually thought to have emerged in the twelfth century.[4] Most of these are not attached to particular authors, and are considered to belong to folk theatre rather than to literati dramatic writing.[5] Around the Yuan–Ming transition of the mid-fourteenth century, *nanxi* evolved into what would become a dominant dramatic genre, the *chuanqi* 傳奇 (literally 'legend') dramas. It is in this form that the canonical dramas of the late Ming and early Qing – *Peony Pavilion*, *The Palace of Everlasting Life*, *The Peach Blossom Fan* – are written. By and large, *chuanqi* are more literary in style than *nanxi*, are credited to particular elite authors, and are often thought to represent the moral view of literate elites rather than those of ordinary people. *Nanxi* narratives were later adapted to this style, and the versions that one now sees on the *kunqu* stage, for instance, generally exhibit greater literary and ideological orthodoxy. The documentary bias against folk theatres probably obscures the widespread

18 LIYUANXI – CHINESE 'PEAR GARDEN THEATRE'

continuation of *nanxi* narratives in less altered forms. In Fujian, such drama texts fell into oblivion, and 'but for the discovery of some random copies in European and Japanese libraries we would not even suspect that plays in the regional language were printed as early as the sixteenth century', making them until recent decades a largely 'forgotten literature'.[6]

Little wonder then that there was excitement in the second half of the twentieth century when scholars, motivated to research proletarian culture and with access to newly rediscovered historical scripts, found that the repertoire still performed in Fujian showed links to the written *nanxi* corpus. In 1986, the distinguished scholar Liu Nianzi 劉念茲 (1927–2010) even went so far as to claim that Fujian was the birthplace of *nanxi*.[7] The scholarly consensus has strongly approved another of Liu's ideas – that genres such as *liyuanxi* represent a continuation of *nanxi* repertoire and to some degree also performance practice – but has declined the Fujian-origin hypothesis. Instead, Wenzhou's claim to being the cradle of *nanxi* is usually accepted, with attention directed to the historical record to find when these narratives and performance practices might have reached Fujian.[8]

One of *liyuanxi*'s principal claims to historical importance in a broader theatrical context is the preservation of *nanxi* narratives and elements, and the so-called 'four great southern drama' narratives all have a narrative expression on the *liyuanxi* stage.[9] Unlike later versions of the same narratives, which rewrote them according to their own developing stage conventions, *liyuanxi* versions retained the practice of naming the play after the main character.[10] In general, the process from southern drama to *liyuanxi* appears to include the retention of the main plot and the characters, with compression of the text and adaptation to the musical demands of the genre.[11] Seventeen plays in *liyuanxi* repertoire correspond to lists in the important Ming sources on *nanxi* repertoire. The evidence of sources such as *Account of Southern Drama* (*Nanci xulu* 南詞敘錄),[12] *The Correct Beginnings of the Nine Modes* (*Jiugong zhengshi* 九宮 正始) and other related texts tend to suggest that the repertoire entered the Quanzhou region in the early Ming, around the late fourteenth century.[13] The relationship between *liyuanxi* and *nanxi* is corroborated by close similarities between fragments of *nanxi* text such as those collected by Qian Nanyang 錢南揚 (1899–1987) with those given by the actor accounts of traditional repertoire recorded in the 1950s.[14]

The majority of early southern Fujian theatre and song texts deal with the Chen San and Wuniang story. This is also true of theatre and song texts from Chaozhou, the closely related cultural area that provides the other setting of the story, since the male protagonist Chen San is a man of Quanzhou, while his beloved Wuniang is a maiden of Chaozhou. Comparison of early Chen San scripts with the transmitted stage tradition shows the repertoire texts and the stage performance to be intimately related and in some passages all but identical.[15] The first script that must be considered as an ancestor to *liyuanxi* practice is a 1566 edition of the Chen San and Wuniang narrative titled *Lijing ji* 荔鏡記 (*The Story of the Lychees and the Mirror*), known by the reign under which it was published as the Jiajing edition.[16] Other old scripts instead call the text the *Lizhi ji* 荔枝記 (*The Story of the Lychee Branch*).

The Jiajing edition, like the rest of the corpus long forgotten, became known in recent decades largely through the efforts of the National Taiwan University scholar Wu Shou-li 吳守禮 (1909–2005). In the 1950s, Wu found and reproduced two copies with scholarly apparatus, one from Tenri University in Japan and another at the Wylie Collection of Oxford's Bodleian Library.[17] A Shunzhi era version (1644–61) of the same story, also preserved in Japan, reached Wu in 1965.[18] Finally, several copies of an 1884 version were compared and reproduced by Wu in 1978.[19]

Building on Wu's work was the important recovery of three Quanzhou theatre and song texts, containing a greater diversity of repertoire, discovered by Piet van der Loon in Dresden and Cambridge, and reproduced alongside van der Loon's substantive introduction in 1992. Of the recovered texts, *Mantian chun* 漫天春 (*All-embracing Spring*), a 1604

20   LIYUANXI – CHINESE 'PEAR GARDEN THEATRE'

dramatic anthology of eighteen scenes, known from a single copy in Cambridge, where it has been held since 1715, is the most important.[20] The most recent addition to this slender corpus of texts is another Ming edition of the Chen San story found in the National Library of Scotland, first described in a 2019 dissertation by Yibo Wang, and close in date and perhaps from the same publisher as *Mantian chun*.[21] The late imperial puppetry, song and theatre texts from nearby Chaozhou form a closely related and even less-researched literature.[22]

FPLET staff consult *Mantian chun* when considering what pieces to revive or reinvent. The collection represents an archive of pieces that can be considered authentic and traditional whether or not a performance tradition is active or in human memory. In *Mantian chun*, scenes are brief, and no single narrative is represented by more than three scenes, which suggests that performances in the seventeenth century might have been primarily scene-based rather than composed of single long narratives. That practice of performance of scenes rather than full narratives continues to be common. As early Minnan printing, the texts have also attracted the attention of linguists, whose analysis supports the claim that they show 'hybridization of native and alien strata in a linguistic system', suggesting that narratives had already become deeply acculturated in the Minnan region by the end of the Ming.[23] At the same time, some of the scenes collected in *Mantian chun* can also be incorporated into nationwide narratives of dramatic development, as has been done with the naughty nun narrative 'Si fan' 思凡 (Longing for the Secular Life).[24]

Before the foundation of the People's Republic in 1949 and the establishment of state troupes shortly afterwards, scripts were probably seldom used by actors, most of whom were in any event illiterate. Repertoire before the PRC shows little sign of being influenced or altered by literati text,[25] with the entirety of the traditional repertoire being passed down by oral transmission, and no play being associated with a named author. Thus, while a portion of scripts has been passed down to the present, much of the traditional repertoire is known to us in print only through an early PRC process, when actors orally recounted their repertoire to intellectuals assigned to the new troupes upon the establishment of the troupes. These versions form the basis for the *liyuan* scripts in the *Quanzhou chuantong xiqu congkan* 泉州傳統戲曲叢刊 (*Quanzhou Traditional Xiqu Collectanea*; 1999/2000), filling nine of the work's fifteen volumes.[26] Many of the original manuscripts are still held by the troupe.

It was comparisons of these scripts with fragments that generated the broad consensus that Fujian genres (including also the neighbouring Putian genre *puxianxi* 莆仙戲) have conserved elements of *nanxi* that were largely eliminated by literati versions of the same narratives. All three of *liyuanxi*'s constitutive tendencies contain *nanxi*-derived repertoire pieces such as *Zhu Wen* 朱文, *Lü Mengzheng* 呂蒙正, *Su Qin* 蘇秦, *Wang Shipeng* 王十朋 and *Liu Zhiyuan* 劉智遠.[27] These stories have become canonical for the genre, the troupe and indeed for Hokkien theatre more generally.[28]

Performance records in the region

As is often the case with theatre, some of the earliest relevant records come from detractors. For instance, while in Zhangzhou, the great neo-Confucian philosopher Zhu Xi 朱熹 (1130–1200) appears to have forbidden puppet theatre out of concern for the morals of the local people. His disciple Chen Chun 陳淳 (1159–1223) elaborated his views on the immoral aspects of theatre, writing in 1197 of the region's 'vulgar custom' of performing 'licentious plays ... in densely populated areas and busy thoroughfares' and thereby harming the public.[29] However, such early materials are insufficient to provide a solid connection to genre.

By the mid-sixteenth century, both 'official' (Mandarin) 正音 and 'dialect' (Hokkien) 鄉音 styles of singing were recorded, an indication that more than one genre was being practised and that regional mobilities were in play.[30] He Qiaoyuan 何喬遠 (1558–1632) noted that Quanzhou

22 LIYUANXI – CHINESE 'PEAR GARDEN THEATRE'

people were fastidious about correct pronunciation.[31] Child performance in 'local' *tuqiang* 土腔 music is recorded from the Wanli era, eliciting, as accounts of performance often did, expressions of moral concern from local officials. Perhaps the best source, dated 1605 or 1606, is from the official Chen Maoren 陳懋仁, who writes

> As the boy-actors are attractive, wealthy families get hold of them without grudging the high price they have to pay. These boys have made it their daily habit to wear the [effeminate] cicada hairstyle and to powder their faces. But they all sing in the local idiom, and I do not understand the meaning. To amuse myself I used to have someone interpret it for me, but I did not keep it up. Previous to this, a certain clique raised the matter as being harmful to good morals and advised that the authorities should take it in hand.[32]

Chen goes on to note that the families who owned the boy actor troupes were crafty and powerful enough to overcome any attempts to suppress the practice. Other terms indicating locality besides *tuqiang* include 'Quanzhou melody' *quanqiang* 泉腔, and suggest that a theatrical practice was already distinctive in terms of music and dialect. More than two hundred years later, the official Lin Feng 林楓 (1798–1864) not only remarked on the presence of boy theatre troupes in Quanzhou, but similarly complained about the incomprehensible dialect.[33] Evidently, generations of officials from outside the region were mystified by this dialect theatre.

The practice had evidently spread to Taiwan by the time a late seventeenth-century Zhejiang traveller, Yu Yonghe 郁永河, noted 'down south' performances at a Mazu temple in Tainan.[34] The theatre was still common another two hundred years later, in the Japanese colonial period, when it was often called *laoxi* 老戲 ('old theatre'),[35] and Taiwan's first modern historian Lien Heng 連橫 (1878–1936) takes explicit note of the 'lesser Pear Garden' in his account of theatre in Taiwan, observing that singing was in Quanzhou Hokkien and plots involved romantic tales of parting and reunion.[36]

LIYUANXI HISTORY 23

Perhaps the performance of children accentuated the animus against theatre among local officials. In about 1815, judging the Chen San narrative to be licentious, a Xiamen magistrate called Xue Ningdu 薛凝度 banned child actor performance of the narrative.[37] By the late nineteenth century, *liyuanxi* was suffering from competition of troupes from outside of the area, including Jiangxi, with local troupes meeting demand from the lower end of the financial spectrum.[38] An 1856 Quanzhou temple inscription records a stage being built for both for 'lesser Pear Garden' and for plays in Mandarin, and similar records are noted from the same time in Tainan, in southern Taiwan. Shi Hongbao 施鴻保, a minor administrator, wrote in his *Fujian Notes* (*Min zaji* 閩雜記) of the mid-nineteenth century about the popularity of boy actors who 'sing all sorts of indecent songs' and 'still dress like girls and walk about in the town'.[39] Later in the nineteenth century, references in poetry suggest that performances of the narrative were mixing Chaozhou and Quanzhou dialects.[40] In response to market demand, at least one child actor troupe began performing *jingju* alongside the 'lesser Pear Garden' repertoire.[41] By the late nineteenth century, boy actors were probably more common than the 'greater Pear Garden' adult counterparts in both Fujian and Taiwan, perhaps due in part to their generic flexibility. Records of particular troupes and actors, rare in the nineteenth century, become more common in the first half of the twentieth century and in some cases begin to connect with the lineage of actors who would be assembled for the FPLET after the foundation of the PRC.[42]

Performance technique and stage movement are even more difficult areas to trace than script fragments, since stage elements are not typically committed to paper. Though scholars like Wu Jieqiu 吳捷秋 (1920–2008) have highlighted similarities that can be demonstrated or inferred between the performance practices of historic southern drama and *liyuanxi*,[43] there is probably not enough material either in *nanxi* scripts or surrounding performance to fully establish such kinetic genealogies.[44]

Liyuanxi in the modern era

Like other aspects of Chinese culture and society, *xiqu* was destabilized by contact with the West in the late Qing and the Republican period. Thrust into competition with Western spoken theatre, *xiqu* lost its synonymy with the stage itself. Gradually, it became merely the national, traditional form of stage arts in a century in which Chinese intellectuals had an enduring and violently recurring suspicion of Chinese tradition as well as an urge to make it 'scientific', 'correct' or 'modern'. Since that period, substantial effort has been devoted to creating models of *xiqu* performance that would be 'appropriate for the times' by adjusting gender roles, musical systems, stage construction, set and prop conventions, theatre education and, not least, commercial models. *Xiqu* reform in various proposals and incarnations has been on the table for over a century, and is usually stated as a matter of survival for the art.

Fujian was not nationally at the forefront of twentieth-century intellectual developments in China, and Hokkien culture had and retains a reputation for conservatism.[45] Emigration of men to Southeast Asia transformed the Quanzhou region to a substantial extent into a remittance economy while also creating a market for Hokkien theatre abroad. In theatre terms, this means that neither the experimentalism nor the mass media associated with the theatre world in large urban societies were characteristic of Hokkien theatre at this time.

Instead, we have evidence of continued performance, both ritual and commercial, locally, in Taiwan, and in the Southeast Asian diaspora. Scattered records attest to repertoire performance and troupe movements. Poetry by the late Qing Quanzhou scholar Gong Xianhe 龔顯鶴 mentions 'southern melodies' where the '*Lychees and the Mirror* are circulating all through the towns', suggesting that *liyuanxi* or a related genre was being performed at that time.[46] Taiwanese newspapers of the Japanese colonial period (1895–1945) sometimes record

LIYUANXI HISTORY

that '*liyuan* was sung and performed' or '*liyuan* was sung and performed in celebration', suggesting that the adult 'greater' Liyuan forms were performed on the island during the colonial period, likely until the Kominka movement (1937–45) suppressed or Japanized local performance culture. Troupes also began to travel to various parts of the Hokkien diaspora. One 'lesser Pear Garden' children's troupe of about thirty members, called Double Pearl Double Phoenix (Shuangzhu feng 雙珠鳳), performed to sold out houses in Manila in 1924. The New Girls' Troupe (Xin nüban 新女班) achieved success in Singapore in 1925, furnishing what may be the first record of repertoire performed by all-female troupes. Oral history interviews in 1980s Taiwan with elderly people who had been child actors before the war captured some of these stories:

> At first the Double Pearl Double Phoenix [troupe] sang only southern melodies, there were three boys and five girls bought from Taiwan, and a very old teacher of deep artistry was hired to come to Xiamen to set up the troupe. The theatre was in Tuqi 土崎 [Alley] in Xiamen, and we rehearsed seven-children ensemble [i.e. lesser Pear Garden ensemble] repertoire. Performances were all for religious processions.[47]

Already before the war, however, *liyuanxi* was fast losing preeminence among Hokkien theatregoers to other genres: the Double Pearl Double Phoenix Troupe upon return to Xiamen hired a Taiwanese teacher and switched to *gezaixi* before leaving again for Surabaya in East Java.[48]

Liyuanxi in the first half of the twentieth century can perhaps best be sketched by considering the biographies of actors who became the first performers of the post-1949 troupe. Born between 1892 and 1921, they had been child actors. Several such actors, such as Cai Youben 蔡尤本 (1899–1974), who would become the troupe's first director, had been sold into itinerant theatres as children. Another key figure in the setting down of the traditional repertoire was Xu

Figure 1.1 *He Shumin, the singer of one of the first* liyuanxi *recordings and a pioneer female performer. Image by courtesy of the FPLET*

Zhiren 許志仁 (1898–1968) who was the best-known *chou* 丑 (clown) performer of the *xianan* tradition, and ensured that much of the comical repertoire of the theatre was set down. Women, long absent from the tradition, not only entered but also became prominent in theatres. Most famous among these was perhaps He Shumin 何淑敏 (1918–87), a major transmitter of *shanglu* tradition, as well as the actor recorded singing on one of the earliest vinyls of the musical tradition, a 1957 excerpt from *Su Qin* (Figure 1.1).

The following generation includes some of the oldest *liyuanxi* actors now living, trained as children before 1949. They recall having begun their stage careers without a formal learning process, having simply been put onstage as children in the 1940s before being integrated post-revolution into the new state theatre.

By all accounts, before 1949 actors in the region barely eked out a living. Occupying the lowest rung of traditional society, actors lived hand to mouth on the demand for theatre created

Figure 1.2 *Xu Maocai* 許茂才 *(1903–80), a* dan *from a* xianan *troupe, participated in training the first PRC generation of performers. Image by courtesy of the FPLET*

Figure 1.3 *The clown Yao Suqin* 姚蘇秦 *(1919–92) was sold into a troupe at age nine and as an adult transitioned to 'greater Pear Garden' repertoires. After 1953, he taught all three* liyuanxi *tendencies. He appears here in the role of Yitong in* Yitong Settles the Rice-Cake Accounts (Yitong suan guo zhang 義童算粿賬). *Image by courtesy of the FPLET*

by rituals and celebrations. Actors were largely illiterate; one performer remarked that 'in the old [i.e. pre-1949] society, acting was [a profession] for those with no other choice'.[49] Actors did not work from written materials, and training and performance were structured around obedience to teachers,

LIYUANXI HISTORY

who were sometimes also older relatives. The formalization of theatrical practice as part of the PRC's official state culture would constitute a fundamental transformation of actor status and theatre structure.

Foundation and consolidation: The troupe in the early PRC

Theatre reform was an important element of cultural policy in the early PRC. Repertoire reform was accompanied by an equally fundamental change that concerned the formalization of genre integration of the troupes into the new state's institutions. New generic categories were overlaid on a complex series of related practices, which in many cases created new genres as much as it identified existing ones.[50] *Liyuanxi* was one such genre, created by drawing new boundaries around old practices as the PRC 'set about folding all theatre into the framework of the state apparatus by registering, categorizing and domiciling performance troupes and personnel'.[51] Though the early years of the PRC constituted a period of wholesale restructuring in Chinese theatre and adaptation in response to government directives, it is increasingly clear that there was a great deal of regional variation in policy application as well as grey areas within that policy.[52] In Quanzhou, even the name of the new genre and troupes had to be determined, since the troupe drew on three heretofore institutionally separate practices with their own conventions and repertoire.

A major founding intellectual and artist-administrator of the troupe was Xu Shuji 許書紀 (1914–2008), who came to the task of establishing a new theatre with experience both in wartime patriotic theatre and as an educator in Chinese schools in the Philippines.[53] Xu, having become head of the Jinjiang County Palace of Culture (Jinjiang xian wenhuaguan 晉江縣文化館) in 1951, helped assemble the actors of the three traditions for the purpose of organizing and continuing the tradition in 1952, giving the troupe the name Jinjiang

County Great Liyuan Experimental Theatre (Jinjiang xian da liyuan shiyan jutuan 晉江縣大梨園實驗劇團). In 1953, as part of the nationwide ongoing theatre consolidation, the Ministry of Culture authorized this troupe to be amalgamated with the Jinjiang Prefecture Cultural Worker Team (Jinjiang zhuanqu wengongdui 晉江專區文工隊), creating the Southern Fujian Experimental Troupe (Minnanxi shiyan jutuan 閩南戲實驗劇團). In 1958, the troupe's name was changed to the Fujian Province Liyuanxi Experimental Troupe (Fujian sheng liyuanxi shiyan jutuan 福建省梨園戲實驗劇團), the name by which it is still commonly known today. Although the details of the various names may be of limited interest, the history of troupe names between illustrates how somewhat diffuse *nanxi*-based practices slowly coalesced around the name *liyuanxi*.[54] The genre's name outside the PRC and its boundaries with other genres have remained fuzzier: in Taiwan the dominant name has been derived from the musical practice *nanguan* 南管 ('southern pipes') and is therefore called *nanguanxi* 南管戲 ('southern pipes theatre').

Cai Youben, the troupe's first director, was fifty years old at the time of the establishment of the PRC in 1949. He hailed from an impoverished rural background and was recognized by the party-state as a victim of the 'old society', having been sold into opera performance as a ten year old.[55] After he aged out of that theatre, he had become a chief percussionist, in which role he learned the ins and outs of a wide range of repertoire. Actors such as Cai, trained in various role types and having taught actors for twenty years before the revolution, provided the performance knowledge for a theatre practice that was largely unwritten. The actors of this cohort were also the principal teachers for all the pre-Cultural Revolution actors, instructing over a hundred students. The seventy or so plays that were fixed in the amalgamated genre's repertoire at this time are thought to represent only a fraction of those being performed in the Ming and Qing dynasties.

As intellectual cadres committed the knowledge of actors such as Cai to paper, they also tailored repertoire for the spirit

LIYUANXI HISTORY   31

of reform, shortening the texts and making them ideologically more suitable.[56] Much of this work was undertaken by Lin Rensheng 林任生 (1912–72), a Quanzhou native and since 1930s a member of the Chinese Communist Party, with a background as an author and director of political theatre for children.[57] Scripts were reformed to suit the new performance environment. Scenes that showed sympathetic protagonists as mendacious or philandering were trimmed to clean them up, and all manner of sexual or otherwise coarse humour was expunged. Another founding member of the troupe was Wu Jieqiu who forged distinguished careers as a stage director and academic. He first set *liyuanxi* on a path to PRC success as stage director of the revised *Chen San and Wuniang* and in later years laid the foundations of scholarship on the genre.[58] In 1954, the troupe, performing a version of *Chen San and Wuniang* as revised by Xu, Lin and others, would achieve success at the Eastern China Opera Observation and Performance Convention (Huadong qu xiqu guanmo yanchu dahui 華東區戲曲觀摩演出大會) performances in Shanghai, an event which for the first time brought several regional theatres to national attention.[59] The prizes and repute won with the performance of the revised *Chen San* script continue today to be a major touchstone for the FPLET at a national level, almost sixty-five years later.

The chance to perform on the national stage was extraordinary for the actors of the period, the genre theretofore being practically unknown outside of Quanzhou. It was apparently the first time that the genre was performed in Mainland China outside of its native province.[60] This success represented an evolution from local performance, much of it in rural communities for ritual occasions, to a presence also on the national stage. It also meant direct contact with central cultural authorities and major academic institutions who incorporated the genre into a national vision of diverse regional theatrical expression while eliminating offensively 'feudal' repertoire. For a northern theatre director and drama critic such as Zhang Aiding 張艾丁, the performance

32 LIYUANXI – CHINESE 'PEAR GARDEN THEATRE'

represented 'a bumper harvest from the theatrical frontlines'.[61] The national reception of the performance immediately drew a connection to the *nanxi* roots of the genre,[62] including in terms of repertoire, lexicon, prosody and instrumentation. By this time, the idea that *liyuanxi* owed its distinctive performance style to relative isolation from the greater trends in Chinese theatre had also taken hold, and gave the FPLET standing as an ancient and relatively exotic genre.

Further successes were to follow: a 1955 performance series in Beijing brought praise from one of the Ministry of Culture's leading figures, Zhou Weizhi 周巍峙 (1916–2014).[63] The staging of the newly found *Zhu Wen* manuscript was a success, as was the adaptation of the Zhu Bian 朱弁 story as *Cold Mountain* (*Lengshan ji* 冷山記) in 1959. The latter received a warm reception from the national theatre establishment in Beijing due to its patriotic themes.[64] Though changes to *liyuanxi* performances was part of a wide-ranging repertoire reformation based on practical and ideological considerations, productions such as *Zhu Wen* raise the possibility that where the written record was relatively weak, as in Quanzhou, the impacts of such reform may have been especially strong.[65]

The successes of the mid-1950s raised the genre's profile in official circles, and further cohorts were recruited in 1959 and 1960, mostly from rural families who hoped to improve their children's prospects by placing them in state education and employment. In the early 1960s, there were three troupes performing *liyuanxi*, with Quanzhou's twin city of Jinjiang and the more rural area of Nan'an, to the west of Quanzhou both maintaining troupes. Together, the three theatres employed something like 200 people.

Cultural Revolution

Like almost the entirety of theatre in the PRC, these troupes fell victim to the Cultural Revolution. Soon after its outbreak in 1966, all three *liyuanxi* troupes were disbanded. In the period's vicious environment, actors occupied an ambiguous position – by and large their family backgrounds were humble, but on the other hand they were professionally committed to an art that could be construed, in those uncompromising times, as feudal and anti-revolutionary. Actors who were not selected for the cultural propaganda teams were often the subject of political persecution, and some of the retired actors were publicly humiliated and others killed in the turmoil. Even the more fortunate younger actors lost their homes in apartments in urban Quanzhou (which had been allotted through the now-disbanded troupe) and were transferred to the countryside, where they worked in factories and farms.

As the worst of the turmoil receded in 1969, a portion of the *liyuanxi* actors were organized into five cultural propaganda teams (*wenyi xuanchuan dui* 文藝宣傳隊) which staged the various revolutionary shows and sketches as well as some of the famous revolutionary opera stories, adapted for Quanzhou dialect and *liyuanxi* music. The Jinjiang cultural propaganda team became a troupe again in 1974, gathering together most of the actors of the former *liyuanxi* theatre company. Here, too, ideological pieces predominated until traditional pieces were once again permitted from 1977.[66] Politically safe pieces included an adaptation of Lu Xun's *Diary of a Madman* (*Kuangren riji* 狂人日記) and *Wandering through Green Mountains* (*Ta bian qingshan* 踏遍青山), inspired by a Mao poem.[67] These shows are now never performed in their entirety, although arias from the revolutionary opera *Azalea Mountain* appeared in the troupe's 2019 National Day celebration of the PRC's seventieth anniversary.

Post-Mao

After the Cultural Revolution, professional *liyuanxi* theatre again went through a series of names and configurations before the present single troupe was firmly established.[68] The troupe's name, the Jinjiang District Liyuanxi Theatre (Jinjiang qu liyuanxi jutuan xiju jutuan 晉江區梨園戲劇劇團) from 1977, would be changed in 1985 back to the FPLET.[69] In 1977, as traditional repertoire was becoming authorized once again, an intake of new students at the theatre school was also permitted. The first revival of 'traditional repertoire' was an adaptation of *Fifteen Strings of Cash* (*Shiwu guan* 十五貫), considered to be ideologically relatively safe, since the *kunqu* version had been praised by Mao Zedong and Zhou Enlai.[70]

By this time many of the pre-1949 veterans of the theatre, including Cai Youben, had died. Numerous other old actors had retired, unwilling or unable to return to the troupe after the Cultural Revolution. This changing of the guard brought new personalities to the fore. A key figure for the transition to the post-Mao era was Su Yanshi 蘇彥石 (1928–2011),[71] who had entered the troupe in 1954 but made his most important contributions in this period as the initial stage director of the new scripts by Wang Renjie. He was also a mentor to the future troupe director and leading actor Zeng Jingping; it was he who first recognized her talent, giving her a key role in a 1980s staging of *Zhu Wen*.[72] In 1988, when Zeng Jingping was only twenty-four, Su announced in the pages of *Theatre News* (*Xiju bao* 戲劇報) that she was 'the best actress in Fujian',[73] highlighting her role in Wang's *The Chaste Woman's Lament* (*Jiefu yin* 節婦吟 1987; revised 2006) just as that play was once again bringing the troupe and genre to national prominence.

Nor was attention confined to the PRC. As early as 1980, the troupe began to receive invitations to tour. Eight performances by a fifty-nine-member group in Hong Kong that year, at the invitation of the local Quanzhou émigré institutions, represented the first post-Cultural Revolution visit of a PRC troupe to the British colony.[74] The troupe's reputation was further enhanced by 1983 and 1985 shows in Beijing, not to mention an October 1985 tour of Japan, where their shows were also televised. In an administrative change that same year, the troupe regained provincial company status, a further indication of the troupe's rise in fortunes.[75] The early 1980s are recalled by many as one of great vigour and popularity – the troupe performed their marquee play *Chen San and Wuniang* for three months running without changing venues – although actors still earned only a very modest salary.

In the later 1980s conditions improved as the troupe was in high demand and the market economy gathered force. Performance fees rose after every Lantern Festival, and the FPLET (in tandem with Xiamen's Jinliansheng Gaojia Troupe 廈門市金蓮升高甲劇團) always set the yardstick by which the other troupes in the region measured themselves. Competition was strong, motivating actors to borrow narratives from other genres, such as *chaoju* in the Chaozhou region. The FPLET had two performance teams, often operating at the same time, both touring the countryside.

The prominence and prosperity of the genre, which began in this period and continue to the present, are closely associated with two figures just mentioned: the playwright Wang Renjie (1942–2020) and the actress and troupe director Zeng Jingping (b. 1963).

The death of Wang Renjie in May 2020 marked the end of an era for *liyuanxi* and perhaps for *xiqu* scriptwriting in general. Although he had a long and storied career, his reputation rests principally on his work as playwright for the FPLET, and his oeuvre is closely associated with the revival of the genre's fortunes in the post-Mao years.

Born in 1942, Wang was part of a generation of authors and intellectuals whose careers were profoundly marked by the caesura of the Cultural Revolution, though he would become known for showing a path for *xiqu* playwrighting to emerge from the ruins. The most important period of his creation followed his return from Shanghai to Quanzhou in the early 1980s. Becoming the troupe's resident playwright, Wang authored a series of plays that have remained in repertoire and gained recognition as some of the best efforts at contemporary playwrighting for traditional genres. Wang's six major scripts for the FPLET were *Maplewood Evening* (*Fenglin wan* 楓林晚; 1984), *Chaste Woman's Lament, Chen Zhongzi* 陳仲子 (1990), *Scholar Dong and Madam Li* (*Dongsheng yu*

Figure 1.4 *Wang Renjie. Image by courtesy of the FPLET*

Lishi 董生與李氏; 1993), *The Yamen Runner and the Female Thief* (*Zaoli yu nüzei* 皂隸與女賊; 1998) and *Cai Wenji* 蔡文姬 (2002). Wang was never prolific, his six major works for *liyuanxi* being written over almost two decades, and his collected dramatic works are available in a single volume. Although a lively and voluble conversationalist as well as a wide-ranging thinker, his essays too are few, far between, and written in an old-fashioned, erudite style.

In one such piece he reflected on his first memories of *liyuanxi*, remembering watching performances at the homes of wealthy relatives from his earliest years.[76] Steeped in *liyuanxi* and traditional culture from a young age, the aesthetics, rhythms, pacing, role types and prosody of *liyuanxi* were second nature to Wang. As a dramatist, his works were hailed for their adoption of tradition, the convincing use of traditional metre and register, their dramatic structure and their accessibility to audiences. His allusiveness, spanning the entire range of classical China and of local culture, is highly unusual for a contemporary playwright. The stage conventions of traditional *liyuanxi* too are largely observed in his work, such as the appearance of the *sheng* (scholar) role before the appearance of the *dan* (female); the bare stage and very economical use of props, and the techniques of *zibao jiamen* 自報家門 (self-introduction of characters), *dingchang shi* 定場詩 (scene-setting poems), *zibai* 自白 (self-explanations), *pangbai* 旁白 (aside) and *bangqiang* 幫腔 (off-stage 'helping' chorus).[77] With the traditional uncluttered stage, the conception of the pieces is actor-centred and contains long monologues more focused on developing emotion than building suspense.

At the same time, Wang wrote with knowledge not only of the tradition but also of Chinese and Western spoken theatre, the *xiqu* dramas of the Republican era, the revolutionary operas of the Cultural Revolution and the development of other *xiqu* forms both in the PRC and in the broader Sinophone world. Western theatre's influence is easily discerned in the basic structure of the plays, with their single-evening and conflict-centred plot with development, climax and resolution. Another modern element is a willingness to break the fourth wall: on one famous occasion in *Scholar Dong and Madam Li*, as the main characters have left the stage to consummate their passion, a dialogue is staged between the percussionist and another musician, providing commentary on this sudden turn of events.

As the critic Lü Xiaoping points out, Wang Renjie's reputation as a leading playwright of a traditional stamp was established while he retained these Western-derived concerns with dramatic structure. In an interview, Wang commented 'when we read many of the Ming and Qing theatre masterpieces, it's very hard to identify how much there is of that discrete dramatic structure, conflict and contradiction, climax, etc. according to the Western spoken theatre mould ...' and proceeded to suggest that their worth was in their aesthetics, grace and emotive exploration.[78] When his later work – such as *Chen Zhongzi* – dispensed with the kind of conflict and dramatic development *xiqu* had borrowed from Western models, the critical response was much less positive.[79]

As architect of the troupe's success, the only comparable figure is the current troupe director Zeng Jingping. Born in Quanzhou in 1963 to spoken theatre actors, Zeng has for three decades been both the troupe's lead performer and since 1999 the troupe director as well. She has also been a member of the National People's Congress since 2003, an unusually high political position for a theatre artist.[80] The key female roles that are mentioned in this book – the traditional roles of Wuniang and Zhu Maichen's wife, as well as the newly written roles of Madam Li (*The Scholar and the Widow*), Madam Yan (*Chaste Woman's Lament*) and Meng Yuehua – have all featured in her core repertoire.

Having grown up around theatres, Zeng was performing small roles onstage by the age of five or six. Her parents, having experienced the persecution of artists during the Cultural Revolution, were wary of the stage life for their daughter. Zeng consequently signed up for the recruitment exam without informing them, and enrolled in the first post-Cultural Revolution cohort to enter the theatre school, in 1977. At the time, she recalls, 'I didn't know what *liyuanxi* was, I just knew it was some kind of art'.[81] Having completed her training, she joined the FPLET in 1982, but initially, being neither physically nor vocally obviously well-suited to any given role type, she was assigned a wide variety of characters, an experience of uncertainty and adversity that she would later credit with fostering her versatility and resilience.[82]

It was Su Yanshi who mentored and cast her in larger parts, having perceived her artistic instincts and work ethic. By the mid-1980s, she was a standout young performer, even as the Deng Xioping era's rapid improvement of economic prospects in Quanzhou meant that few of her cohort remained in the theatre. In 1989 she became the first Fujian winner of the Plum Blossom Prize, China's highest honour for theatre performers. Her second Plum Blossom Prize in 2008 secured her place in the highest echelon of performers nationwide, this honour having been granted to only thirty theatre artists nationwide between 1994 and 2007.

Zeng's performances draw praise for their psychological acuity combined with technical skill.[83] She has been noted for pushing the limits of the depiction of women in the traditional repertoire as well as in the genre's contemporary, original scripts. Her depiction of frustrated desire in *The Chaste Lament* or of a righteously triumphant liaison in *Scholar Dong* provides intertextual complication of the traditional maidenly roles of the genre, such as Wuniang. Recent work as a stage director, both at the FPLET and in other troupes, has further revealed the wide scope of her talents.

Liyuanxi and society

Recruitment and training

Actors were a stigmatized group before 1949. The official attitude towards actors became more benevolent and paternalistic in the early PRC. The *xiqu* reform movement of the 1950s granted actors status as cadres as well as urban household registration.[84] Much of the attraction of performance in a troupe has, since that time, depended on recruiting rural students with a promise of a better standard of living due to secure state employment and the promise of city life. Alongside the rise in status naturally came also the wholesale institutionalization of theatre at the levels of both genre and troupe.

The changes made the profession more attractive: in the first three decades of the PRC, performers in state troupes overwhelmingly remained affiliated with theatres from entry into training in early adolescence until retirement and even after. Genre transmission was one of the principal concerns throughout the history of the troupe and thus educating a younger generation of performers was a priority once the institutional framework stabilized after the 1954 success. Theatre education, long an informal though often harsh process conducted in troupes, was turned into a state project. The first cohort of children was recruited for theatre school in 1956 at the Jinjiang Region Arts School (Jinjiang diqu yishu xuexiao 晉江地區藝術學校), later to be named Fujian Province Quanzhou Art School.[85]

That founding cohort numbered between twenty and thirty students, most of whom completed the training and progressed to the troupe. Salaries for professional actors were low but income was stable, and stage performance could for the first time be considered a respectable profession. One performer of that cohort remarked 'at the time nobody thought that much about it, we just thought we've got work, the state gives us a salary, we had security, we were very satisfied, people's lives got a lot simpler too, it never occurred to me to go anywhere else'.[86] Actors had to push their own carts, laden with costumes and props, through the countryside for tours. They set up the stage in the morning; did political study in the afternoon; performed in the evening; and sometimes helped with farm labour, washing in streams when possible.

When the troupe regrouped after the Cultural Revolution, China's social and political system had begun to undergo rapid change. The 1977 intake consisted of approximately thirty-five students, who graduated in 1982. This generation's adolescence coincided with the beginning of the reform period, and, as one performer remarked, 'the entire population went into business ... all of our classmates left'. The troupe being short on actors for performances, recruitments were also made in 1978 for immediate training in the troupe rather than in the school. Because of a number of further departures during the schooling period, a supplementary small intake occurred in 1980, with actors graduating in 1983. This generation too lost several performers due to family dispersal to Hong Kong and Southeast Asia, a sign of the resilience of Hokkien transnational connections in the face of the new openness of Deng Xiaoping's China.[87] Others remained in Quanzhou but left the theatre to do business, work as civil servants, or – in one case – to teach in a *wushu* school. By 1992 and 1993, performance frequency had slowed considerably, largely because the actor pool had shrunk so badly, even as audience demand remained high. A performance in the countryside might net only CN¥100 for the troupe, with each actor receiving CN¥5; with the economy booming, this level of income was becoming unattractive to young performers. In the early 1990s, troupe finances were parlous: salaries were not paid for extended periods of time; the troupe might even borrow money from wealthier troupe members, to be repaid at interest. Many actors took on second jobs, even if they formally remained members of the troupe. The graduation in 1993 of a supplementary intake (recruited in 1989) of over thirty actors permitted normal operations for a while, but within five years all but a handful of these had left too. Today only one man and three women of this generation remain in the troupe.

The liberalization of the economy and the *danwei* 單位 (work-unit) system over the past forty years and the economic development of the southern Fujian region have generated greater options for performers. Never before have actors had such a secure income and a high social status. Government initiatives and prizes have helped the FPLET attract frequent media exposure, and new technologies such as WeChat have mobilized a new fan base whose reach extends far beyond Quanzhou, tapping into other pockets of highbrow *xiqu* fandom, for instance the white-collar *kunqu* fans in the Jiangnan area, many of whom visit Quanzhou during festivals

42 LIYUANXI – CHINESE 'PEAR GARDEN THEATRE'

to attend performances. Tours abroad, once a precious rarity, were occurring annually or even more often until the Covid-19 pandemic brought things to an abrupt halt in 2020. On the other hand, a perceived decreasing work ethic and connection to sources of tradition lead to concerns that the technical foundations of the genre will erode in coming years, particularly as the 1977 generation reaches retirement age and troupe leadership passes to younger generations or to government appointees from outside the genre.

Further full generations of actors were recruited in 1989, 1997 and 2007. The newest cohort is currently in training at the school, having been recruited in 2018–2019, and one of the challenges of the troupe is to ensure that the profession remains attractive enough to retain performers. As with many *xiqu* genres, obstacles to recruitment represent a major threat to genre continuity. There is a concern that – in an affluent region – the career of actor, with low salaries for the young, is not sufficiently alluring to attract the students with the best conditions. The decline of Hokkien speech, due in part both to the arrival of migrants from other regions of China as well as a continued emphasis on Mandarin as the official national language in education and media, means that there are concerns about the ability of newly recruited adolescents to deliver Hokkien lines accurately or take direction in Hokkien.

As elsewhere in the PRC, *liyuanxi* performers are today almost exclusively graduates of dedicated theatre schools who were recruited in childhood. In the words of Zeng Jingping, 'you have to learn the techniques as a child, when the joints are still tender, so that they are fixed that way and can be developed later on'.[88] Consequently, actors who are now in late middle age have worked together since recruitment as pre-adolescents in the late 1970s and early 1980s. All presently active troupe members are drawn from the graduates of the Fujian Province Quanzhou Art School (FPQAS).[89] For *liyuanxi*, students from the dialect area are recruited at the age of twelve or thirteen. Education at these public theatre schools takes from three to six years, during which time students are instructed primarily in *xiqu* technique, with other courses having a decidedly secondary importance. Upon graduation, most students pass performance examinations to become part of the troupe, with which, if they choose, they will remain for the rest of their professional careers and, in many ways, lives. Typically, the decision as to when another intake will be made and the recruitment process undertaken is in the hands of the troupe. Troupe actors visit primary schools, vetting children for physical, musical and performative aptitude to become a *xiqu* actor.[90] Training at school is often only nominally independent from the troupe. The pathway from student to troupe actor is thus a pipeline which, as long as acting as a profession remains sufficiently attractive, determines the professional course of an individual from adolescence to old age.

The generation that was born in the mid-1980s now fills the majority of stage and major administrative roles.[91] Recruited from the region in 1997, none of them had made a conscious choice to become actors. Their mostly rural families had been attracted by the fact that actors are part of an institutional *danwei*, with the implications that this could provide an 'iron rice bowl', including a fixed income and retirement. Students entered theatre school at the age of twelve or thirteen, having completed or nearly completed elementary school. After four years, this cohort underwent two years of further training in the troupe before receiving vocational secondary school degrees (*zhongzhuan* 中專). Of the forty performers (twenty-three girls, seventeen boys) recruited in the 1997 generation, fifteen have left the troupe for other employment, and two have died. Eleven girls and twelve boys from this cohort remain in the troupe. As has usually been the case, the proportion of girls leaving has been higher, since girls who make good marriages are not considered to need to make an income or enter into family businesses; indeed, girls are reportedly also easier to secure for recruitment in the first place, since they are not carriers of the family lineage and are not expected to be main income earners.

Relative to other generations, more of the 1997 intake has remained with the FPLET, since the prestige of the theatre has

44 LIYUANXI – CHINESE 'PEAR GARDEN THEATRE'

increased and the prospect of secure employment has become more alluring as once spectacular economic growth rates have slowed. The feeling among this cohort is largely that the moment of rapid economic expansion concluded before their time. The youngest generation (2007 intake) is only beginning to assess its options, but the early evidence suggests that the local economy is not such a pull factor at this time, and that attrition may remain low in the context of modest alternative prospects.

Despite economic liberalization, many elements of the *danwei* system remain central to actor lives, and the state-funded structure has been integral to the genre's survival. In 1991, there were 140 employees, but state troupes are today considerably smaller than a generation ago.[92] The FPLET, at slightly over a hundred regular employees in 2021, is among the largest theatres in the province. Troupe administration continues to be responsible for aspects of members' lives to a degree not familiar in Western theatrical systems. They must arrange to honour older performers by invitations and visits, serve different fan bases (who are attached to different actors and elements of repertoire) and give younger performers practical main stage experience. In consequence, major productions and festivals have an administrative role: the theatre must prepare material for potential prize competitions for individual actors and productions, and the authorities must be given an account of the theatre's recent work. Programming for major events mines the capital of the genre, tailoring repertoire to the tastes of the various audiences and the means and needs of the troupe.

The construction of the Liyuan Classical Theatre, inaugurated in 2008 and situated a few minutes away from the dorms for unattached young actors, has provided a hub for the company, with canteens, altars, costuming, research spaces, archive, offices, party secretary, accounting, rehearsal rooms, staff rooms, stages and guest rooms all inside its five floors. Numberless tea sets reside in nooks about the theatre, laundry is almost always hanging out to dry, always a drum beating a rhythm or an actor warming up her voice is audible, not to mention the tick-tock of the highly competitive table tennis matches. From the fifth floor one looks out on the public park, the red roofs of the city, and, in the distance, a garish statue of Coxinga. A dovecote is on a roof directly opposite and the flock circles over to visit and veer away. After show nights, seafood and noodles having been commanded to accompany the beer or *huangjiu*, the lively postmortem begins. It is this inhabited quality that attracted the attention of the French director Patrick Sommier, who wrote that 'one lives there each day of the year, celebrating the festivals of the calendar – gods' feasts, Spring Festival, and Mid-Autumn Festival. It's a theatre to be lived in'.[93] Given the way that *liyuanxi* actors have been trained and lodged together since childhood, until recently also in close proximity with their teachers and older colleagues in the same compound, it is unsurprising that the troupe functions also as a little society, and the rhetoric of 'one big family' is taken quite seriously. The kinship terms that are generally present in Chinese educational systems (master-father, study-sister) retain this close familial association.

It is true that the ongoing urbanization of Quanzhou has in the past decade made the city centre less dense, and that the actors are part of a middle class moving out to more spacious apartments in high-rise tower blocks that are outside the urban core (where building height is controlled for heritage purposes). This means that the actors live within thirty or forty minutes of one another and of the theatre, rather than within a quarter of an hour or less. Nevertheless, the shared past and the binds of interwoven professional and personal relations mean that the troupe remains a closely knit group.

Liyuanxi and gender

Despite considerable recent change, *xiqu* society is far from having reached gender parity, whether it is the academic, the bureaucratic or the literary side of things. At the level of theatre staff, in the FPLET as throughout the PRC *xiqu* world, the gender roles remain deeply ingrained – men for stage tech, lighting, sound; women for costumes and make-up. Within *xiqu* companies, the area closest to achieving parity is, unsurprisingly, on the stage itself, where women necessarily provide a great deal of the star wattage. This is particularly pronounced in *liyuanxi*, where the contemporary repertoire has been strongly geared to women's stories. It is therefore perhaps not surprising that the women who are most prominent and powerful in PRC *xiqu* companies have first reached prominence in their capacity as performers, with a number of women capitalizing on their stardom to occupy major positions in the government organizations and professional societies that administer *xiqu*.[94]

As is the case with other types of theatre in China, *liyuanxi* performance was principally undertaken by men and boys during late imperial times, although girl and women performers had entered the genre by the early twentieth century. Still, most *dan* performers were men until the 1950s, at which point they passed their roles onto female disciples – as in other genres, the practice of men performing as women has all but ceased professionally. It has remained common to train women to perform the genteel scholar, and there is acceptance for such performers throughout the *xiqu* world.[95] The mid-century also saw the advent of women playing the scholars' roles. One of the major interpreters of these roles both before and after the Cultural Revolution was Cai Yazhi 蔡娅治 (b. 1938), who entered the troupe upon its foundation in 1953 and was for many years a leading performer of the central role of Chen San. On the other hand, there are no longer any men who perform women's roles, except as part of comic relief, where clowns may represent hideous women.

Furthermore, while none of the prominent women of *liyuanxi* self-describe as feminists or adopt its rhetoric or stances, it is noteworthy that the female-centred rewriting of *The Pavilion of the Imperial Stele*, for instance, introduced at greater length later in this book, became possible because a female troupe director had given a young female playwright the opportunity to realize a new vision of traditional repertoire that interprets old narratives from contemporary mores.

Diasporic *liyuanxi*

The geographic reach of the Hokkien diaspora ensured that *liyuanxi* and related genres have been performed not only in its native province of Fujian, but also in Taiwan and in Southeast Asia. Records before the mid-nineteenth century are spotty, but until the Second World War tours in the region were a common occurrence, with recent scholarship doing much to deepen the understanding of genres of performance and areas where such troupes performed.[96] Early travel abroad mostly took the form of commercially motivated troupes meeting community and temple network demand. Most of this Hokkien theatrical circulation outside the core area of Fujian and Taiwan, however, would have been from the genres of theatre that were more popular in the early decades of the twentieth century, that is *gaojiaxi* and later *gezaixi*, as well as the puppet troupes. Today, Hokkien theatre in general struggles for survival in the Southeast Asian diaspora, with the highbrow *liyuanxi* no longer well known even to communities with well-defined Hokkien identities and cultural practices, such as those in Penang, Medan or Manila.

Not so in the 1980s. In the early post-Cultural Revolution period, Hokkien diaspora interest in the reconstituted FPLET represented a definite benefit for the troupe. The longest such tour undertaken by the troupe was from 20 October to 20 November 1986, to Manila, when the troupe was invited to the Palace Opera and Film Center (Huangdu yingjuyuan 皇都影劇院), with the coordination of the Philippine Cultural Center and the participation of thirty-one Philippine-Chinese organizations as auxiliary sponsors. The driver of the project

48   LIYUANXI – CHINESE 'PEAR GARDEN THEATRE'

was a Philippine Hokkien magnate called Zhuang Dingshui 莊鼎水. On behalf of the hosting committee, he wrote in the audience programme that he hoped the theatre could prove itself 'a cultural "angel"' for improving relations between the Philippines and the PRC, then only recently established. Fifty-five members of the troupe undertook the trip, performing twelve different shows over thirty performances, including one to commemorate the 120th birthday of Sun Yat-sen.[97]

The performances largely featured the abridged versions of traditional *liyuanxi* troupe fare such as *Chen San and Wuniang* and *Li Yaxian*, although there was notably (since it is not a usual play for the genre) also an adaptation of the *kunqu* play *Shiwu guan* (Fifteen Strings of Cash). The use of Chinese in the programme suggests that the expected audience for the shows was predominantly ethnic Chinese, but the performances also attracted a high level of official interest from the Philippine state. The programme includes messages from then President Corazon Aquino, with the usual hopes for 'greater cooperative efforts by our two peoples'[98] and one from Vice President Salvador H. Laurel, speaking a little more ominously about the need for cultural exchanges in the Cold War, since it was an 'age when so much conflict is spawned'.[99] Messages follow from the PRC ambassador Chen Songlu 陳嵩祿 and Chinese Filipino associate Supreme Court justice Pedro L. Yap, who watched performances and whom troupe members visited in person.[100]

It is clear also that the event engaged much of the organized Manila Chinese community: the hosting committee lists over 100 names, and 31 organizations are thanked in Chinese on the inside cover of the programme, the majority of them Manila Chinese community organizations, including place name associations, Hongmen, business groups and friendship associations. After the premiere at the Cultural Center, the remaining shows were held at the Asia Theatre (Yazhou xiyuan 亞洲戲院). Performing over a dozen productions for thirty-one performances in twenty-eight days in October and November, the troupe's visit (fifty-five people, including thirty-one performers and eleven musicians) elicited dozens of enthusiastic articles in the Manila Chinese-language press,[101] including both reports of shows and other activities as well as some explanatory pieces authored by troupe members, such as Wu Jieqiu. The troupe leader Xu Zaiquan 許在全 contributed a poem inspired by the reception of local alumni associations and reprinted in several other outlets, and local Sinophone author Huang Chun'an 黃春安 wrote verse about how he was moved by the performances. The troupe in its entirety stayed at Zhuang's three-story home on Ong Pin Street, in the core of Manila's Chinatown. The Fujian newspapers also made a brief note of the trip, as did the *People's Daily* overseas edition.[102] The Manila-based *Shijie Ribao* 世界日報 reported that the audience was 'intoxicated' not only by the charm of the performance but also 'on account of hearing the sounds of their hometown'.[103] For many of the troupe members, it was the first time they had travelled abroad.

The Manila trip represented an important step in building the national and international profile of the troupe and improving the financial health of the troupe. With the reinstatement of cross-Strait travel, playwrights and scholars began to exchange ideas and performance troupes with Taiwan, resulting not only in the 1990 visit of a Taiwanese *nanyin* theatre troupe led by Chen Mei-O 陳美娥 but also to a dedicated major Taipei conference in 1997 organized by the theatre scholar Tseng Yong-yih 曾永義. The 1990s and 2000s would see continued engagement with the diaspora, including a fifty-one-strong contingent visiting Singapore in 1991 for seven performances.[104] In 1997, a nine-performance, fifty-eight-person trip constituted the first time the troupe made a commercial trip to Taiwan. In the 1991 and 1997 trips the troupe performed not only core traditional repertoire such as *Chen San and Wuniang* but also Wang Renjie's *The Chaste Woman's Lament*,[105] suggesting that *liyuanxi*'s reputation for excellent contemporary *xiqu* was spreading beyond the mainland.

Related traditions in Taiwan and Singapore

The process of consolidation of older actors from different tendencies into an official troupe never occurred in Taiwan. During the period of one-party rule and martial law (1949–87) under the Kuomintang (KMT), only Mainland-derived forms of theatre such as *jingju* received funding and support. Among Hokkien genres, the popularity of *gezaixi* and the puppet genre *budaixi* survived to become symbols of Taiwanese identity, but *liyuanxi* was a small minority practice. By the 1960s, the genre was moribund on the island.

During that period, it was impossible for Taiwanese artists to communicate with theatrical practice in the PRC. Close cultural ties were, however, maintained by the Hokkien of Taiwan and those of the Philippines, which was also a US ally and where the KMT exercised considerable control over the Hokkien Chinese community. In Manila, *liyuanxi* had been sustained in local societies, not least due to the work of Quanzhou performer Li Xiangshi 李祥石 (1912–2003), who, intending to perform in the Philippines for three months, had been trapped there in 1939 by the outbreak of war. These associations were not satisfied with the quality of their own performances and so they struck upon the idea of recruiting girls from Taiwan as performers. Representing a group led by the Silian Musical Studio (Silian yuefu 四聯樂府), Li travelled to Taiwan in 1963 looking to recruit students for 'lesser Pear Garden' repertoire, in which work he was assisted by Taiwanese *nanguan* societies. Ultimately fourteen girls participated in training, aged from fifteen to seventeen, and mostly from near Tainan, where the group was trained. Without this Philippines-based initiative, *nanguanxi* would likely already have vanished from Taiwan.[106]

The girls were trained in Taiwan from February 1963, and first took to the stage in spring and summer 1964, performing scenes in Tainan, Kaohsiung, Taichung and Taipei, and featuring on Taiwanese television in November and December of that year.

In 1965, they left to perform in the Philippines for four months, arriving for the Spring Festival performances in February. They regularly performed afternoon and evenings (three to three and a half hours for each performance). Supervision was so strict that they left the theatre only three times: to pay a New Year's visit to a community leader, to visit the zoo and to go shopping before their return to Taiwan. Because their repertoire was limited, they not only had to perform the same plays repeatedly, but also had to supplement their 'lesser Pear Garden' repertoire with *gaojiaxi*. Upon return to Taiwan, having fulfilled the troupe's purpose of entertaining the Manila Hokkien, the troupe disbanded.[107]

Several of the individuals, however, continued to be active on the stage in Taiwan. Among the students in this cohort was Wu Su-hsia 吳素霞 (b. 1949) who had joined over the objections of her family. In 1966, Li Xiangshi fell out with the Silian Musical Studio (Silian yuefu 四联乐府) and he lost access to their scripts. Li and Wu returned to Taiwan to have all the scripts transcribed anew by the elderly performer Xu Xiang 徐祥 (1887–1968), who was from Taiwan, and had been sold into servitude as a boy actor at the age of six.[108] Li made frequent trips between Taiwan and the Philippines, winning several awards from the ROC government for his work in cultural transmission in the 1980s, before moving to Keelong permanently in 1996.

Since 1967, Wu (sometimes also credited with her married name as Lin 林) has been teaching in Taiwan and has been the chief activist for the continuing small-scale amateur existence of *nanguanxi* in Taiwan, generally with the support of ROC government theatre or traditional arts mechanisms. Founded in 1993, she leads the Haphe Academy (Hehe yiyuan 合和藝苑) in Shalu, which features regular performances, at times using the term *nanguanxi* and at other times *liyuanxi*. It has received a modest amount state funding since 2000, and institutions that support the genre or provide venues include the Changhua County Museum of Traditional Nan Bei Music and Theatre (Nanbeiguan yinyue xiqu guan 南北管音樂戲曲館) and the

Taipei National University of the Arts (Guoli Taibei yishu daxue 國立臺北藝術大學), where Wu has also taught. In 2009, Wu was named a Carrier of Cultural Heritage by the Taichung city government.[109]

At 2019 performances of scenes from *Chen San* that I attended, there were thirty people in the audience for the ticket-free show, and a similar number involved in the performance as musicians, technicians and performers, so the scale of the genre's reach is small. The productions represented an end-of-semester performance for Haphe students. Some students know how to sing *nanguan* but are not performers, while others are dancers learning to sing. State support schemes subsidize teachers and students for the classes over four-year periods. Wu's Haphe Academy is the only group in Taiwan that seeks to be traditional in its choice of repertoire, treatment, costume, music and so on. This Taiwanese strain of transmission through the Philippines has resulted in the retention of some pieces of repertoire that are no longer performed by the FPLET, and also means that none of its practices bears the marks of the 1950s PRC reforms.

There are other groups that draw on the stage tradition, some of which have evolved from orchestral *nanguan* ensembles. Taiwanese artists have sometimes sought to 'take an elitist route and transform it into a modern theatrical art form; *nanguan* is subjugated to dance as an accompaniment rather than remaining a self-contained art form'.[110] This creates another genre of *nanguan* theatre, which, though separate from *liyuanxi* in terms of training and institution, is closely related by narrative and music. Theatrical *nanguan* productions tend to be quite experimental, since they seek to invent theatrical modes of performing a vocal tradition. Examples of Taiwanese troupes have included interpretive dance to the poems of Yu Kwang-chung set to *nanyin*, incorporation of Japanese *butoh* dance, and collaborations with European directors on classical Chinese themes.[111]

One of the most prominent such groups has been Chen Mei-O and her Han-Tang Yuefu 漢唐樂府 group, which drew on *nanguan* music to theatricalize various narratives of classical China, several of which also toured Europe.[112] Chen had visited Quanzhou in the early post-Mao period, and much of the group's performances have used traditional repertoire and performance practice as a basis for further creation. One well-known performer with Han-Tang was the Quanzhou-born and trained Wang Xinxin 王欣欣 who married a Taiwanese husband and established her own workshop which produces orchestral and semi-theatrical *nanguanxi* shows on a modest scale. Another group which performed *liyuanxi* repertoire and indeed both organized trips to Quanzhou and invited FPLET instructors to work in Taiwan was the Gang-a-Tsui ensemble (Jiangzicui juchang 江子翠劇場) based in the New Taipei neighbourhood of that name since 1993. Though their training mixed Western theatre pedagogy with the methods learned from Quanzhou, several of the productions were of traditional repertoire, including of the core *liyuanxi* play *Zhu Wen*.[113]

A parallel emergence of theatre out of *nanguan* practices occurred in Singapore's Siong Leng Musical Association, whose transnational activities have included complex stagings for European consumption that effect a 'deliberate conflation of "ancient" tradition with new age mysticism' by claiming 'a deeper Buddhist and spiritual underpinning behind *nanyin* and traditional Chinese culture at large'.[114] In order to be able to represent Singapore, it has also been 'deliberately localized and improved with a Singaporean flavour in its infusion of South Asian and Malay elements drawn from the cultural fabric of the island-state'.[115] Siong Leng has in recent decades managed to assemble funding and receive support from diverse but mostly state sources in Singapore, ultimately benefiting from the city-state's desire to improve its international cultural profile.[116] As with the FPLET and Han Tang Yuefu, some of the greatest sources of international recognition have come from France.

From a Quanzhou perspective, these groups in Taiwan or Singapore may be acknowledged as a derivation of a shared musical source, but these practices are differentiated from

54   LIYUANXI – CHINESE 'PEAR GARDEN THEATRE'

liyuanxi both by the absence of a connection to traditional stage practices and lineages and the substantial alterations made to the music. Overall, the differing fates of *liyuanxi* in the PRC and traditional *nanguanxi* elsewhere are best understood as a result of the state-led art system operational in China versus the much less centralized (though still state-subsidized) systems in Taiwan or Singapore. The latter more closely resemble Western countries insofar as many small arts groups survive, not always very long, on a mixture of public grants, ticket sales, private sponsorship and unpaid work.

International connections

In the twentieth century, theatre has formed a major part of Chinese cultural diplomacy, and the approbation of foreign audiences is an important way of validating *xiqu* practice. The bulk of attention has gone to Republican-era tours abroad, such as those of Mei Lanfang and Cheng Yanqiu; it does not seem that the theatre and music culture of Fujian played any part in the representation of Chinese culture outside of diasporic networks until the post-Mao era. Beyond commercial tours, migrant community performance and cultural diplomacy projects, *liyuanxi* has in recent decades toured abroad through the networks of international theatre institutions, including festivals and auteur-driven cross-cultural theatre.

The 1990s first saw the expansion of *liyuanxi* touring to a wider sphere. *Liyuanxi* was first seen outside of Asia in September 1990, when the troupe was invited to Sicily, first as part of the celebrations of the Premio Mondello in Palermo, and then to Rome.[117] A 1991 conference on southern drama and Mulian 目連 opera in Fujian, with performances from the FPLET and other local troupes, brought this family of theatres to renewed attention to Euro-American and Japanese scholars.[118] The first integration of *liyuanxi* into what may be called cross-cultural theatre was likely through the projects of Singaporean director Ong Keng Sen (b. 1963), whose *The Global Soul – The Buddha Project* toured Europe and Singapore between 2003 and 2006. Ong, travelling constantly due to his work as curator for the Berlin Arts Festival, was drawn to the Buddha story as a way of working out the answer to the question 'where am I when I travel so much?' The result was a collaboration between seven artists from various, mostly Asian performance traditions, creating (in the words of the director) 'seven parallel journeys bound together by electronic music'.[119] Ong and promotional materials exceeded even the usual maximum historical estimates by describing the genre as 'a thousand-year-old Chinese operatic form'[120] and pitched the show as an exploration of Buddhism and an example of decolonized intercultural theatre, although some critics found the show to be 'a series of individual performances held loosely together by an exceedingly ambiguous and indistinct theme of travel (and Buddhism)', while others found it to be 'an encyclopaedic undertaking: five different ways of linking the present to cultural memory are braided together'.[121] Ong was especially taken with Zeng's rendition of 'The Great Melancholy', and her performance in *The Global Soul* was based on that scene.

Though a high-profile international collaboration, Ong's auteur interest in *liyuanxi* involved only a single actor, Zeng Jingping. The largest-scale and most sustained encounter of *liyuanxi* with the international theatre world occurred in the mid-2010s, due largely to the efforts of Patrick Sommier, from 2000 to 2015 the artistic director of MC93 (Maison de Culture 93) in Bobigny, on the outskirts of Paris. Having worked for several years with the Peking Opera School in Beijing, in 2012 he arrived in Fujian on a theatre scouting trip, looking for a new *xiqu* project. The troupe performed *Scholar Dong* for him, and he found it a 'very great art, both sophisticated and popular'.[122] In rallying French theatre critics and theatregoers,

56   LIYUANXI – CHINESE 'PEAR GARDEN THEATRE'

Sommier could rely to some degree on the enthusiasm shown in that country for *nanyin* for over thirty years.[123]

In 2013, Sommier returned to Quanzhou with a larger group, including the distinguished Chinese-French translator and intermediary Pascale Wei-Guinot and younger Chinese-speaking director Sarah Oppenheim, to plan what would become a first European tour in 2014 (of Sommier's own theatre at MC93 near Paris, the festival Nuits de Fourvière in Lyon and the Hellenic Festival in Athens). The tour was repeated with *The Chaste Woman's Lament* in 2015 (under the auspices of MC93, which was under renovation, but with the cooperation and at Paris's prestigious Cartoucherie venue of Théâtre du Soleil). In preparation for the 2015 season in France, a delegation of journalists visited Quanzhou, resulting in reporters from France's core culture media all writing profiles on *liyuanxi*, preparing the ground for a wide media reception of the Paris shows in the French press. For instance, *Le Monde* proclaimed that the 2015 performances proved that one 'shouldn't be afraid of Chinese theatre' or *jingju*-derived clichés surrounding 'hours of incomprehensible martial situations' and that the FPLET 'undid stereotypes in a marvellous way',[124] while *Télérama* focused on the way that Zeng 'strangely, magically, manages to perform always as though between words, between gestures. In an ineffable space that becomes unreal and infinite'.[125]

In 2016, upon retirement from the directorship of MC93, Sommier founded a new company called Arts des Nations (a pun in that AdN coincides with the French acronym for DNA) to spur theatrical cooperation between France, China and Russia. That year, he brought a group to Quanzhou including the directors David Lescot and Jean René Lemoine as well as six young actors to study *liyuanxi*, performing French versions of key scenes from *Scholar Dong* and *Chaste Woman's Lament*. The final performances occurred in the presence of leading figures in Quanzhou local government as well as French cultural attachés from Beijing and Guangzhou. Sommier saw in the exchange an opportunity for European theatre to genuinely interact with a fundamentally different theatre in a project 'not guided by the economy or the standardization of cultural products'.[126]

Sommier's efforts produced several other collaborations with French artists, also taking place between 2015 and 2017. Georges Lavaudant, a well-known director and long-time head of Odéon–Théâtre de l'Europe, came to Quanzhou to direct the lighting for several shows including the premiere of *The Imperial Stele* and the revival of Wang Renjie's *Chen Zhongzi*. In 2017, at Sommier's invitation, the young composer Benjamin Attahir sojourned in Quanzhou to work on a composition for the troupe orchestra and one performer. Using an aria from the *Chen San and Wuniang* scene 'The Lesser Melancholy' (Xiaomen 小悶) as his basis, Attahir mixed a Western soprano and a violinist into his piece.[127] What new international tours or collaborations will emerge after the Covid-19 hiatus remains to be seen.

2

Performance foundations and style

Aesthetics and technique

Performance night at the Liyuan Grand Theatre: it may be almost any Saturday of the year, or it could be a weeknight during one of the heady festival seasons. Upstairs, prayers have been offered to Marshal Tian and incense has been lit. In a large dressing room full of mirrors, actors are dabbing on their make-up, climbing into costumes, arranging their headdresses, looking for their sashes. Reflections *en abyme*, voices echoing down the theatre's corridors – warming up, singing, shouting for a piece of costume or a drink of water. Actors and staff, momentarily free, gather in clutches around Quanzhou's perpetual tea services. In the canteen beneath, the engine room of the theatre, the workers have been preparing enormous vats of food for the whole company. In full make-up and in fractions of costumes people crowd around the tables to slurp noodles, spear pork, inhale the salty Hokkien rice. A few have wandered out to the loading dock to smoke in the half-light.

Out front, the audience drifts in through the plush vermilion seating, exchanging the noisy reunions of the grand lobby for the hush of the velvet interiors. The lights dim; the usual

PERFORMANCE FOUNDATIONS AND STYLE 59

bans on videography are solemnly proclaimed. Now chiming percussion, soft and persistent, then the almost tentative pluck of the strings, now starting to insist. Presently the flutes join in, slowly, tugging the music out of the pre-theatrical void. The stage is dark, but now a voice, too, emerges lamenting, wandering, curling. The melisma of the music lends it an air of patience, of endurance, of probing emotion rather than of plot-driven pacing. Soon perhaps a foot, tresses, pale features will appear from the edge of the stage or else will be revealed by the slow dialling up of a lighting cue, a person to articulate the lament, simple robes to speak of the hardship. More often than not, *liyuanxi* begins with a thread of emotion, not with the drums and trumpets of narrative. The orchestral conversation deepens: interrogative percussion pattering, the poignancy of the strings, now growing substantial in the winds.

And the heroine onstage, a widow, pallid face against dark modesty, with only the most sombre adornments. The audience, their knowledge of the plot presumed, expects neither an evolution of character nor the excitement of rapid reverses – instead the experience is one of expansion, the unfurling of a particular emotion, the vertical delving into sorrow and yearning rather than the horizontal unspooling of time, the lyrical moment more than the narrative drive. The focus on longing, often paired with hardship or abandonment and a moral commitment to chastity and fidelity, may be the main aesthetic distinction of the genre.[1] The role of theatre in communicating and maintaining moral standards, a frequent claim of the theatre's apologists, is very clear in the traditional repertoire, which is full of impossibly moral officials and chaste heroines and widows.

Wang Renjie, one of the pithiest commentators of *xiqu* in general and of *liyuanxi* in particular, wrote in slyly deprecating terms about his home genre's aesthetics, deliberately choosing an anthropomorphizing 'she' to sketch the genre:

She speaks in Quanzhou dialect, sings Quanzhou melodies, and outside of southern Fujian and Taiwan it all sounds like gobbledygook. Her traditional repertoire is mostly 'out of date', the stories are simple, there are few characters, the stories contain no big ups and downs. And performance is conventionalized in the extreme, the rhythm is slow, extraordinarily melancholy ... in seven hundred years historical culture and art have undergone enormous changes, but she stubbornly refuses to change, she looks just the same.[2]

This fond account goes some distance to capturing the allure of *liyuanxi*. Wang, who has been among the most successful of all *xiqu* playwrights in creating new dramas, nevertheless always imagines *liyuanxi* aesthetics in the first instance as a continuation and protection of tradition.

In *xiqu*'s modern discourse, this combination of the physical and the vocal within particular conventional constraints underwritten by an important technical heritage founded in early education has often been called an 'integrated art form' (*zonghe yishu* 綜合藝術).[3] *Liyuanxi* shares with other forms of *xiqu* numerous structures of stage practice and aesthetic principles, but also instantly strikes seasoned Chinese theatregoers as distinct. It offers what one prominent French critic called 'the almost physical pleasure of a theatre carried by the complete harmony of prosody, singing and [orchestral] music, which combines the sophistication of a codified genre with great actor freedom'.[4]

In its integration, and in all its elements – movement, repertoire of texts, vocal production, musical system, orchestra composition, prosody, thematic focus, set and props practice – a measure of continuity can legitimately be identified as 'tradition'. It is this technical continuity (differently constituted by each genre) that generates the attributes of *xiqu*. These attributes in turn set *xiqu* squarely apart from other forms of theatre as a genre. The purpose of the preservation of tradition (and the justification for state subsidy) is therefore 'not to make fossils of the past .... but to integrate safely into the present those parts of the past that continue to have meaning for the current age and .... for future generations',[5] even when an appeal to 'age-old tradition' is a rhetorically convenient shorthand.

The genre's slow pacing and focus on the romantic and civil rather than the martial is broadly in keeping with southern genre aesthetics, and represents a distinction from the more acrobatic and bellicose elements of northern repertoire. Emotion tends to be central; plot develops slowly and resolution is often delayed without suspense being a main concern. Psychological response to a quandary or a dilemma tends to be the means of enlisting audience sympathy. A scene may be about waiting for the beloved or pondering an important decision (with the action that occasions or results from the situation occurring offstage). The relatively rapid progression of action and the precipitous resolutions of Western theatre forms seem hectic when compared to the *liyuanxi*'s slow consideration of emotion and leisurely resolutions. In the end, plots typically reach a happy end, although this may occur after death.[6]

Stage motion

Liyuanxi performance is distinct not only in terms of music, dialect and repertoire but also through its physical movements. The foundations of physical techniques are known as the 'eighteen techniques' (*shiba kemu* 十八科母).[7] These are the physical patterns which underlie *liyuanxi* physical theatre, and generate a physical vocabulary, operating within fixed conventions, of a distinct set of postures and movements. One famous rule of thumb theatrical axiom instructs the actor to move so that their 'hands rise to the eyebrow, separate at the level of the navel, point at the level of tip of the nose, and clasp at the level of the chin'.[8] Certain scenes depicting festivities or mendicant performers appear to have absorbed dance movements and sometimes melodies from folk practices.

Liyuanxi movement techniques fill a whole book of the *Collectanea*. Though they cannot be treated in any detail here, certain highly distinctive movement patterns, such as the gaits

62   LIYUANXI – CHINESE 'PEAR GARDEN THEATRE'

of the *dan* role type, can serve as examples. One instantly recognizable way of walking is the 'heart-press gait' (*anxin xing* 按心行; Fig. 2.1), in which the performer holds her thumb and forefinger together high on the right side of her chest; it has no equivalent in any other *xiqu* form. Similarly distinctive is when the *dan* walks with her hands dangling at her sides, called the 'hanging hand gait' (*chuishou xing* 垂手行). Hand positions, too, are unique to the genre, including the 'eagle-talon hand' (*ying zhao shou* 鷹爪手), the 'ginger root hand' (*jiangmu shou* 薑母手) and the 'crab-hand' (*pangxie shou* 螃蟹手). On the other hand, the acrobatics much associated with 'Chinese opera' in the foreign imagination are not prominent in *liyuanxi*, although certain clowning scenes require much agility and grace, and the influence of *jingju* after 1949 has left a small legacy of martial scene practices.

In *liyuanxi*, as in other genres that draw on a long history, performance practice is generated from the consensus attributes – the technical capital – of the genre. Mastery of the technique which constitutes these attributes is instilled during training. That technique is situated in a corpus of narrative systems, having been historically orally transmitted through the disciple-style learning. This furnishes a technical foundation that transmits repertoire in the first instance but that is also capable of being productive of new repertoire, or of reviving repertoire with no living performance tradition. Repertoire then becomes the vessel and archive of technique.

For any given performance, this reservoir of technical options and field of aesthetic constraints is always subject to the decisions of a creative team, which inherits older changes and must make alterations, cuts and additions. The result, as Wang Renjie notes, is that the post-Mao generation of actors 'far from making no changes' was responsible for developing an artistic practice that fosters the 'rescue, transmission, and new shoots' of the genre.[9] At the same time, the actors who embody these new roles and revive old pieces, or the playwrights who created new frames and situations for the exposition of these techniques, have every right to be considered both guardians of tradition and innovative contemporary artists.

Figure 2.1 *Li Hong* 李紅 *and Lin Qiuhan* 林秋韓 *demonstrate the 'heart-press gait'. Image by courtesy of the FPLET*

Role types

Liyuanxi features seven role types (*hangdang* 行當; Fig. 2.2), some of which can be further subdivided.[10] These basic categories have been present from the earliest southern drama and were reflected in Hokkien theatre as early as *Mantian chun*.[11] It is also the seven-role system which gave the 'lesser Pear Garden' boy actor ensembles their most common name, 'seven-child troupes'. The role types in *liyuanxi* are closely related to the systems present in other genres of *xiqu* performance practice,

Figure 2.2 *Student actors in the seven role types in the fifth year of theatre school, c. 2002. From left to right: sheng, wai, dan, jing, tie, mo, chou. Image by courtesy of the FPLET*

although several martial subtypes familiar from northern theatres are either absent or less utilized.

Role types are indicated in all pre-twentieth-century *xiqu* scripts, and in the script usually take the place of characters' names (although important characters also perform a self-introduction disclosing their names upon entering onstage).[12] The importance of a given role type may vary according to which of the three streams of repertoire it emerged from. For instance, the female roles are of much greater consequence in the romantic repertoire than in the moralistic *xianan* plays. Role-types and sub-role types indicate social status, age and gender and come with a reasonably fixed costume. Early in schooling, role types are assigned on the basis of their voice, capacity to move and physical characteristics. Types entail specific codes for movement and voice production, and therefore training is largely provided by teachers from the student's own type.

PERFORMANCE FOUNDATIONS AND STYLE 65

Traditionally, role types fix gender and age of the character but not of the performer. Men playing women no longer occurs professionally, though there are several women who perform male roles, with particularly the young scholar (or boys) often considered appropriate for a young woman to play.

These features lend role types a certain affinity to stock characters in Western spoken theatre as well as to *Fach* in Western opera. However, as in other forms of *xiqu* these 'individual characters are by no means stereotypical in terms of their values, personality traits, and reactions to the circumstances in which they are placed'.[13] Rather, the role types provide technical parameters within which the individual characters are created.

The fundamental seven role types in *liyuanxi* are:

Sheng 生: The hero of the piece. The lead *sheng* is generally a scholar preparing for the exams, which he either fails or (most often) tops. Numerous *nanxi* plots revolve around him abandoning his erstwhile beloved, and it seems that the recensions of the Ming constitute a literati effort to quell such heresies.[14] But Fujian theatre practices were less intimately connected with the literati rewriting of drama, and this seems often to have resulted in the retention of the fickle, selfish scholar.

In traditional plays, the *sheng* must take to the stage first and immediately enter into the matter of the plot. Subtypes of the *sheng* include the 'gauze headgear sheng' (*shamao sheng* 紗帽生), who has already achieved office, and the 'ripped shirt sheng' (*poshan sheng* 破衫生), who has fallen on hard times.

Dan 旦: A female character of any age but of some social status. In repertoire today, this is the most prominent role type, perhaps due to recent and current performer strength in this role at the FPLET. This type can further be divided into the 'great dan' (*dadan* 大旦), the 'second dan' (*erjiadan* 二架旦) and the 'small dan' (*xiaodan* 小旦). The great *dan* has the largest and most difficult roles and her parts frequently involve solo scenes. The second *dan* largely comprises comic and vivacious roles of more common status. The 'small dan' applies to the roles in the 'lesser Pear Garden' tradition, that is to say the romantic roles for young girls such as Wuniang in *Chen San and Wuniang*, originally performed by children.

Jing 淨: The painted-face character, often a warrior or an immortal.

Mo 末: Mostly older male servants and retainers, this category can also include some minor military figures, or risible characters.

Chou 丑: Comic figures of either sex, including incompetent officials, busybodies and matchmakers, nuns, messengers and manservants.

Tie 貼: Although originally this role referred to maidservants, it has evolved to refer mainly to the elderly *laodan* 老旦 character, often the mother of a main character.

Wai 外: A miscellaneous category, generally for elderly men and some villainous figures.

Liyuanxi speech, music and prosody

Like most *xiqu* genres, *liyuanxi* is divided into sung portions – usually accompanied, occasionally not – as well as recitative, dialogue and orchestral passages without vocal music. Sung portions are usually solo although univocal choral sections also occur, especially offstage at the beginning and end of performances. Typically the vocal and the orchestral line are identical, with percussion punctuating and winds and strings ornamenting the melody.

Liyuanxi music is classified by type. Musicological typology for *nanyin* vocal music also applies to *liyuanxi* arias, with an individual aria being a *qu* 曲 that belongs to a 'tune' (*qupai* 曲牌), which are further grouped into 'tune families' known as *gunmen* 滾門. Arias of the same tune share certain metrical and melodic features but also exhibit considerable variation. A tune family shares the same key and metre.[15] Like *nanyin*, *liyuanxi* is considered to have 108 different *qupai*.[16] Pre-1949 strands of repertoire show musical difference when it comes to *qupai*, with the *xianan* repertoire having the largest number of them.[17]

Liyuanxi music also mirrors that of *nanyin* in the way the *qu* fit into a broader typology, consisting of

> three categories of compositions: the 16 instrumental suites (known as *pu* 譜), the 48 song suites (*zhi* 指), and the numerous individual songs (*qu* 曲). The instrumental suites are mostly programmatic music, depicting flowers, animals, or scenery, while the song suites and the individual songs are narrative or lyrical, with their song texts based on historical stories that have been popular in southern Fukien province for centuries.[18]

Qupai, while imposing prosodic requirements in terms of line length, rhyme and tone, does not regulate note length or pitch. Rather, the prosodic restrictions produce a similar melodic contour which is then elaborated on by actors. Actors then pass the elaborations on to their students. Abstractions or particular versions of the 'tune' may also be fixed for orchestral use.[19] At the same time, *qupai* use also interacts with narrative – with certain *qupai* associated with particular role types, emotions or plot circumstances. In these respects, *liyuanxi* resembles other *qupai*-based genres (e.g. *kunqu*) but less so genres using other systems (e.g. *jingju*).[20] The musical structure provides ready frameworks for music written to new plays, and so the role of the composer for new *liyuanxi* productions is not directly analogous to the composer in Western musical theatres.

Both strings and winds are important in generating the characteristic *liyuanxi* sound which, in the words of the 1954 introduction to *liyuanxi*, is 'mellifluous and harmonious as well as rich with national and local colour'.[21] The core instruments for the *liyuanxi* ensemble are the southern *pipa* or four-stringed plucked lute (*nanpa* 南琶), end-blown bamboo flutes called the *pinxiao* 品簫 and the *dongxiao* 洞簫, the three-stringed lute called the *sanxian* 三弦, a two-stringed bowed fiddle (*erxian* 二弦) and a kind of *suona* 嗩吶 (similar to a shawm) called the *aizai* 噯仔. The *nanpa* is the leading string instrument, and among the woodwinds the end-blown flute predominates rather than the transverse one. Instrumentalists frequently switch instruments during the performance in accordance with the timbre desired for a particular sequence.

It is in the percussion section that the most distinctive feature of the *liyuanxi* orchestra is to be found: the foot-controlled drum (*yajiaogu* 壓脚鼓; Figure 2.3), sometimes known also as the 'southern drum' (*nangu* 南鼓) in which motions of the foot vary the timbre and pitch of the drum. The drummer is also responsible for tempo, and in modern versions may

Figure 2.3 *You Yubin* 尤毓彬, *a member of the troupe since 1996, and chief drummer since 2006. Image by courtesy of the FPLET*

PERFORMANCE FOUNDATIONS AND STYLE 69

furthermore act as conductor, for which reason he is sometimes known by military analogy as 'chief commander'. Secondary percussion instruments such as small gongs and clappers are also used. Modern productions, drawing on the troupe's full orchestra, may further incorporate instruments from other Chinese musical and theatrical traditions (such as the *jinghu*, the northern *pipa*, or the *guzheng*).

Most of the orchestra members are trained in a dedicated class at the FPQAS (parallel to the acting class, though not necessarily recruited at the same time), where the first *nanyin* intake occurred in 1984,[22] although some have received private training and unlike actors most of them entered the school with existing knowledge. Quanzhou is also a centre of the traditional production of these instruments.

Notation for stage and orchestral practices was traditionally both in *gongche pu* 工尺譜,[23] but is now familiar to most musicians only in the mathematical *jianpu* 簡譜 form (based on the Galin-Paris-Chevé system). *Jianpu* is a notation system suited to univocal Chinese music because it takes up less space and can be notated without special paper. *Jianpu* as used in *xiqu* ensembles is generally keyed to a particular note (in the FPLET usually E-flat), with the base note functioning as the *do* in the solfège system, allowing for ease of oral instruction. When singing, FPLET performers are always accompanied by an instrument, predominantly the flute (women) or the *suona* (men). While the principal line is notated, this line does not record the substantial ornamentation made by both performer and orchestras, known as 'decorative notes' (*zhuangshi yin* 裝飾音).

Recitation is considered as important and as challenging as singing. Different registers of Hokkien are in use for recitation, entailing different phonetic systems. There is a formal register called 'literary recitation' (*wen bai* 文白) or 'Confucian speech' (*Kongzi bai* 孔子白) in which speech closely mirrors the written text and resembles Mandarin to a higher degree; it is generally used by officials or others of high status. 'Human recitation' (*renbai* 人白) is used for ordinary speech, and is fundamentally

Make-up, costumes, stages

regular Quanzhou Hokkien, being close to the spoken language, if somewhat antiquated. Finally, 'vernacular-literary recitation' or 'literary-military recitation' (*wenwu bai* 文武白) is a mix of the two registers. Thus, where in a literary recitation the Mandarin *jia* 家 might be used for 'home', in the vernacular recitation the actor will instead refer to *cuo* 厝, the usual Hokkien equivalent. As in other genres, lower-class comical roles use an earthy vernacular, whereas the high-status figures express themselves in the elevated (and more Mandarin) registers.

Make-up, costumes, stages

As with other genres of *xiqu*, costumes are closely linked to role type. Thus, on first appearance, costumes (and gait, and sometimes features of the orchestral accompaniment) immediately provide the audience with information on the sex as well as social and moral status of the character. Noble characters' costumes may be threaded with gold; widows appear in simple dark garments; nuns and mendicants wear their own distinctive headgears. Special designs signal supernatural characters or foreigners. Purely ornamental patterns seem to have come into costuming only in the 1940s.[24] Dependent on local embroidery practices, these designs remained relatively independent from costumes elsewhere. Traditionally, costume trunks had to be packed and placed in a ritualized order related to role types. FPLET productions sometimes place the trunks onstage as a homage to the genre's origin in this itinerant history.

Costuming is relatively sober compared to other forms of *xiqu*, and the gorgeous headdresses and robes of northern theatres feature in more subdued forms in *liyuanxi*. Under the influence of more prominent genres, including *jingju*, *kunqu* and *yueju*, 越劇 costuming began to converge in the post-Mao years to a national norm before increased genre consciousness encouraged a return to more traditional costuming. However, one striking feature is that the *dan* characters did not traditionally wear the water sleeves (*shuixiu* 水袖) that are today otherwise ubiquitous in *xiqu* for high-status characters.[25] Although this means the dramatic flaring and flinging of sleeves of other genres is almost never seen in *liyuanxi*, the absence of water sleeves gives the audience a direct view of the actors' gestures and hand poses throughout. For larger productions, the FPLET now may hire costume designers with national reputations – for instance Shanghai Theatre Academy designer Yu Jian 俞儉 was brought in for the designs of the revival of *Zhu Bian* and the premiere of *The Imperial Stele Pavilion*, while older practices are continued for traditional repertoire.

Make-up, too, occupies a less central function than in theatres of north and central China. The ornate and symbolically significant *lianpu* 臉譜 make-up closely associated with northern genres and with the popular idea of Chinese theatre abroad is not prominent in the case of *liyuanxi*. Indeed, the *jing* ('painted face') role type closely associated with *lianpu* is the least common of the *liyuanxi* roles, and the troupe presently has only two actors who perform in this type. Make-up is deployed for certain specific effects: ghosts have white around nose, lips and eyes, while demons and gods may have more dramatic patterning, but *sheng* and *dan* roles have a basic foundation with a layer of rouge and painted eyebrows; the clowns have white markings on the bridge of the nose and on the lips; and the old *dan* roles appear without make-up.[26]

Like most other *xiqu* genres, *liyuanxi* was until the PRC period acted on a bare stage, with minimal props and set, and the orchestra onstage. It is often said that the small steps taken by the characters are a heritage of historical space constraints. The adoption of the proscenium stage in the PRC period has increased the actors' scope of movements, even as gaits and gesture remain based on tradition. Sets are usually minimal, with the proverbial 'one table, two chairs' of *xiqu* décor being a common arrangement; only the large touring productions are more complex. Props are generally limited to evocative articles: love tokens, fans, musical instruments, brushes and paper.

Watching 'The Great Melancholy'

Let us return briefly to the stage to look at the opening ten minutes of a particular scene in order to offer a sense of how motion and music, singing and recitative fit together in a given case. For simplicity's sake, the scene chosen is 'The Great Melancholy', which involves only a single character, the maiden Wuniang, pining for her beloved. Like many scenes in repertoire, it has both a remote and a recent history, with the scene being part of the narrative of the most canonical piece of repertoire, *Chen San and Wuniang*. However, although this particular solo scene was recounted by the actor Chen Jiajian 陳家薦 (1892–1970) in the 1950s, it was not performed for many decades until 2002, when the troupe director Zeng Jingping convinced the elderly Cai Xiuying 蔡秀英, who had learned the play as a twelve-year-old before the revolution, to teach it to her. The performance practice of the scene being otherwise forgotten, Cai was the only possible means of transmission.

Cai instructed Zeng, the troupe director, to come every day from 3.00 to 6.00 pm at Cai's home. However, as Zeng remembers,

> On the second day I overslept [the noon siesta] and was five minutes late, and it took several minutes of calling her name before Teacher Xiuying came to the door. She stood at the door and calmly told me, it's very hot today, you needn't come, you're famous already, you don't need to learn this scene, go back.[27]

Swallowing her pride, and after much pleading, Cai relented, but the anecdote goes to show both the sensitivities around performance knowledge – many actors would prefer that their knowledge vanished rather than to pass it on to an ungrateful student – and the premium placed on repertoire transmission. In the last twenty years, the scene has become a tour de force for Zeng and for the troupe.

PERFORMANCE FOUNDATIONS AND STYLE 73

As the audience sits, awaiting Zeng's entrance, the credits run below the stage on the title screens, reminding the audience of tradition and transmission. Chen is credited for 'oral account of the script', Cai for 'transmitted teaching', the distinguished troupe clown Xu Tianxiang 許天相 as rehearsal director – then, the musical director and the drummer, and finally the performer. Now the lights come up on a high bed centre stage decked in red, and a nightstand with a lamp on the top rack, stage left. Now we first see Zeng as Wuniang, approaching the front of the stage slowly in rhythm to the slowly accelerating patter of the drum, a subdued gong and the clapper.

Wuniang is dressed simply, in a pale green robe, with two long thin tresses hanging down either side to her ankles, a band around her forehead, swaying gracefully as she walks. Her appearance, is a return to tradition, resumed in the twenty-first century after a half-century of using more ornate costumes based on the nationally popular Zhejiang *yueju* genre. Padding slowly forward, the gait indicative of a well-bred woman (with bound feet), her head is bowed and her face demurely shadowed. She holds her dress up at the knee as if to prevent her slippered feet from treading on it. As the percussion reaches an emphasis, she pauses, raises her hands diffidently one higher than the other, looks up, then reverses the position of her hands, and now leaves the upper (left) hand in a pinching position just above her heart. Now she begins to sing (as the name of the *qupai* appears on the screen) and resumes her slow walk forward.

The free hand sways slowly back and forth as she moves incrementally forward and begins her vocal line, now accompanied by the end-blown *xiao* flute, the percussion falling back into a beat-keeping role until needed for dramatic punctuation later on. The first five characters she sings, 'Longing for the beloved', become, due to the melisma, a 35-second sequence. Never motionless in body, gesture or expression, towards the end of the line, Wuniang brings both hands down in a gesture of sadness, then raises them up to chest level again, sliding one hand across her body to suggest

74   LIYUANXI – CHINESE 'PEAR GARDEN THEATRE'

the passage of time, then bringing it down to her hip and giving a jerk of discomfort to match the end of the second line: 'Yearning has turned to gnawing illness'. The character's sombreness, slowness, diffidence and worry are brought fully into the open – the burden of lovelorn solitude has manifested as illness.

For the next seven minutes, Wuniang travels slowly back and forth across the stage, her expression brightening and gestures animated as she sings of the delights of her first love, then subdued and gloomy as she reminds herself of the anguish and anxiety she faces now, alone and uncertain that her beloved will return. Then, feeling that she ought to go to sleep, she prepares herself to lie down, arranging her coiffure, to the accompaniment of the orchestra. As the orchestra fades out and the drum patters lightly to an end, she sits down on the edge of the bed in absolute silence.

Then comes the first recitation passage, a brief soliloquy conveying a poetic resume of her situation – lonely in her boudoir, she is deeply attuned to the beautiful but uncaring natural environment, and unable to sleep on account of her desperate longing. The lines only lead her back to the conclusion that she cannot sleep, and so having delivered herself of her remarks, she rises again to go to the window and gaze out at the moon. The next forty seconds or so bring back an orchestral melody, this time without the voice, as, weakened by her illness, she rises slowly and laboriously to unlatch and open the window – and is instantly delighted by the beautiful sight of the moon, briefly returning to the vivacity that she had in the earlier scenes of the drama. As is typical of traditional performances of *xiqu*, nothing changes on the stage to indicate the brightness or beauty of the moon, and no prop or set element is provided to indicate the window or its latch. All the changes in mood are the responsibility of the actor, and are legible to the audience through the performer's actions, reactions and voice. In this sense, *xiqu* is perhaps also more novelistic, because we are perhaps more in the mind of the protagonist (in a solo scene) than in other forms of theatre, and the illusion of objectivity much reduced by the spareness of set and props.

These sequences represent only the first ten minutes of the first fifty minutes of the scene, but they are reasonably typical, at least of a *liyuanxi* solo scene, where there is no dialogue and the plot is not advanced. It is the very eventlessness of the scene, the necessity to keep the audience engaged simply through the gestures and postures and vocal modulations of longing that make the scene both so difficult to perform and astonishingly perspicacious about the circular and unresolved nature of yearning. And while Western opera can offer important and interesting parallels such as the 'Letter Scene' in *Eugene Onegin*, any such analogies are not only more full of incident, but they are also shorter than these riveting explorations of amorous longing that are core to *liyuanxi*'s repertoire today. Perhaps no genre so vividly enacts the actual experience of frustrated desire: the alternation of energy and fatigue, of unreasonable hope and unreasonable despair, of the aimlessness paired with the urge for action.

3

Repertoire

Overview

Liyuanxi repertoire today combines plays with origins in tradition (which inevitably also have complicated adaptation histories) and 'newly written' plays (*xinbian xi* 新編戲), which in the case of currently performed repertoire are all but completely scripts dating from the 1980s or later. For traditional repertoire, a common performance format consists of three or four scenes (*zhezixi* 折子戲) combined for an afternoon or (more commonly) an evening's entertainment. Typical scenes last between twenty to fifty minutes.[1] Before 1949, selected scenes would once largely have been performed for weddings, Buddhist and Taoist festivals, and funerals; the full-play format, on the other hand, was more characteristic of non-ritual commercial theatre. The effect of the 'selected scenes' format, which appears to have been common by the early seventeenth century, is that many narratives are familiar not as full stage dramas but as selected scenes.

In a full-play format, a single story is pursued from beginning to end over one performing session or in multiple sessions over several days (either on successive evenings, or else in afternoon and evening sessions). Many lengthier traditional narratives have been adapted for performance at one sitting; these are often the result of 1950s adaptations, which were in turn derived from the dictated recollections of older performers that were then adapted for the needs of the stage of the early PRC and 'corrected' (*jiaodui* 校對), for the most part by Lin Rensheng. Since older performers, including Cai, were illiterate, the process of 'correction' included recording their accounts, transcribing them and making judgments about the written characters (in some places a challenge, given the extensive homophony of Hokkien). These scripts were 'recorrected' (*fujiao* 複校) in the 1990s, mostly by the troupe vice director Su Yanshi, in order to be published in the *Collectanea*, which began publication in 1999.

Thus, the 1950s records that would become the *Collectanea* versions also form the starting point for the stage versions that have later undergone further, often extensive, cuts or adaptations. For example, 1957 work by Lin changed the title of one play from *Zheng Yuanhe* 鄭元和 (the male protagonist's name) to *Li Yaxian* 李亞仙 (the female protagonist's name), while also reducing the thirteen scenes to ten.[2] Also, certain plot elements were borrowed from the better-known (and less local) literary version of *The Embroidered Robe* (*Xiuru ji* 繡襦記), thereby making the text more literary and less earthy, part of a general effort to refine and cleanse *xiqu*.[3] These changes are not visible to most theatregoers today: without knowledge of the specific script and performance transmission history it is hard to pick out what elements derive from a pre-1949 performance script and/or tradition and which are later interpolations. Naturally, some plays transcribed in the 1950s neither have a strong performance tradition nor a large audience following, and so are passing into oblivion, as necessarily is the case given the limited number of actors and performances. Others are known in fragments and may be filled in and revived if the troupe so chooses. Such considerations often have to do with the suitability of certain actors and availability of particular role types, as well as of the tastes of the troupe's senior management (all of whom are current or former actors) and the playwrights.

78   LIYUANXI – CHINESE 'PEAR GARDEN THEATRE'

Newly written plays have absorbed a greater diversity of influences and are less strictly bound by traditional role types. The new 'revolutionary' plays which were composed for political purposes in the 1950s and early post-Mao era are now seldom if ever performed, and almost all pieces still in repertoire and that have been premiered in the last twenty years are costume dramas. Thus, even Wang's early play *Maplewood Evening*, a highly regarded portrait of a widow in 1980s China, has not been staged since 2001.[4]

Compared to other genres of traditional theatre, new *liyuanxi* scripts represent an important portion of repertoire. This is significant not least because of the paucity of scripts often said to afflict modern and contemporary Chinese theatre. Newer plays may also travel better, since they are less likely to contain highly local references or dialect jokes, being at least partly written for a national audience. They are also less likely to reflect an outdated morality, as many of the traditional pieces do. Participation in the various forms of 'little theatre' gives genres such as *liyuanxi* a little more room to experiment, since 'little theatre' is at least theoretically lower budget and does not claim to represent the genre's canon.[5] Even when scripts are original, however, they are written to observe the rules of the genre, and to the *liyuanxi* aficionado a new script will be replete with allusions and imitations of the traditional repertoire, since technique is embedded in the repertoire and vice versa.[6]

The following section offers an overview of common pieces of traditional repertoire in the three tendencies of *liyuanxi* before taking a closer look at six key pieces of repertoire. Of these six, three are of a traditional origin, and three have been written in the post-Mao period: a balance that reflects *liyuan*'s status in Chinese theatre as one of the rare genres of *xiqu* to be equally well known for its new pieces as for its trove of traditional repertoire.

Traditional repertoire is collectively known as the 'eighteen shows'.[7] Each of the three *liyuanxi* constitutive tendencies had

REPERTOIRE

separate (though on occasion overlapping) repertoires, and eighteen is to be taken (as it is with regards to the 'eighteen techniques') as an important symbolic number rather than a precise enumeration.[8] The repertoire shows both how *liyuanxi* connects with the other genres of *xiqu* and those where it is notable for having retained repertoire that is elsewhere lost or little known.

Repertoire derived from the child actor 'lesser Pear Garden' tendency:

Dong Yong 董永 is a version of the well-known *The Fairy Couple* (*Tianxian pei* 天仙配) narrative, concerning a fairy maiden, the daughter of the Jade Emperor, who weds a mortal, Dong Yong. Dong Yong is seeking to sell himself in order to bury his father, an act of filial piety which touches the fairy maiden. She descends to earth in the guise of an ordinary woman, and angers Dong by picking all the flowers in the garden, then astonishes him by bringing the fallen petals back to life.[9] As in other versions of the tale, the fairy maiden is ultimately forced to return to the heavens, where she bears a child from her marriage with Dong Yong. The *liyuanxi* tradition is distinguished by the twist that she is instructed by her own father to return the baby to Dong, since he has ultimately shown his worthiness by topping the imperial exams. The child actors were typically hired to perform this auspicious piece for weddings and for one-month and one-year celebrations of babies' births. In the 1950s, Lin Rensheng changed the motivation of the maiden so that it was instead the coldness of the imperial palace, and not the Confucian virtues of the hero, that lured her down to earth.

Gao Wenju 高文舉, also called in other traditions *The Story of the Pearl* (*Zhenzhu ji* 珍珠記), is a narrative known from Ming scripts, and popular in a number of southern genres.[10] The plot concerns the title character, a student much indebted to his father-in-law. Upon succeeding in the national examinations, Gao is compelled to marry the daughter of the prime minister. When the first wife makes her way to the

80 LIYUANXI – CHINESE 'PEAR GARDEN THEATRE'

capital, she is first pursued by brigands, then imprisoned by the jealous and vindictive second wife. Ultimately Gao discovers and frees her.

Guo Hua 郭華 is known also as *Rouge* (*Yanzhi ji* 胭脂記) and *The Shoes Left Behind* (*Liuxie ji* 留鞋記) and is listed in *Account of Southern Drama*. *Zaju* and *nanxi* versions of the narrative are both extant from around 1600, though likely they are earlier and share a common ancestor with the *liyuanxi* version (as recorded in *Mantian chun* and in the performance practice as recorded in the Cai Youben transcriptions). The plot concerns the scholar Guo Hua, in the Northern Song capital of Kaifeng for the imperial exams. While there, he develops an infatuation with Wang Yueying 王月英, who sells rouge in a store. Repeatedly visiting the shop on the pretence of buying rouge, he ultimately succeeds in arranging a tryst on the Lantern Festival. However, when Yueying arrives with her maid at the designated temple, Guo Hua is drunk from carousing at the festival. He has moreover offended the tutelary deity, who prevents Guo from waking when Yueying attempts to rouse him. Yueying leaves her shoes and handkerchief behind as tokens. Distraught upon awakening, he swallows the shoe and asphyxiates.

Yueying, inculpated by the shoe, is brought to Judge Bao, but ultimately Guo recovers and the happy couple are married. Both the scene of the initial meeting and the temple scene are often programmed independently. A film version – besides the *Chen San* film, the only *liyuanxi* feature film of the early PRC – was produced as *Rouge* in 1959 or 1960 by Hong Kong's Art-Tune Co. (Huawen zhipian chang 華文製片廠). Sadly, the film appears to be lost.[11]

Jiang Shilong 蔣世隆 is a version of the *Moon-praying Pavilion* (*Baiyue ting* 拜月亭) narrative, a romantic *nanxi* story in which the eponymous protagonist, fleeing from the Mongol invasion, meets a maiden in the same predicament. He wins her hand after overcoming obstacles thrown up by parental disapproval.[12] The narrative was included in the early fifteenth-century *Yongle Compendium* (*Yongle dadian* 永樂大典), but

REPERTOIRE

81

has not survived. There are five acts in the *Collectanea* and two in *Mantian chun* as well as a smattering of *nanyin* arias; the Hokkien practice is closely related to the narrative as preserved in a play printed in Nanjing in 1589, *Pavillion of the Moon* (*Yueting ji* 月亭記).[13]

Liu Zhiyuan 劉智遠 is one of the best-known southern drama narratives, better-known as the *Story of the White Rabbit* (*Baitu ji* 白兔記).[14] Liu Zhiyuan leaves his wife Li Sanniang 李三娘 behind when he sets off in a bid for military glory. Persecuted by her in-laws, his wife gives birth to their son in the mill where she is forced to toil. The baby is taken to find his father in the army, and returns sixteen years later (guided by the titular rabbit) to find his mother in 'The Meeting at the Well' (Jingbian hui 井邊會), a popular repertoire scene.

Zhu Bian 朱弁 is based on a Song dynasty historical figure who lived sixteen years in exile among the Jurchen. In the *liyuanxi* version, Zhu refuses the Jurchen princess, living instead with her as brother and sister. When he returns to Song territory, she throws herself in the river. Lin Rensheng reworked the traditional scenes into a version (retitled *Cold Mountain* [*Lengshan ji* 冷山記]) that won praise in Beijing in 1959 by emphasizing the ethnic nationalism of the play while underplaying the romantic plot surrounding the Jurchen princess Xuehua 雪花. The 2009 revival, with Wang Renjie's alterations, sought a happy medium between the traditional and the rewritten versions.[15]

Some narratives reached the contemporary repertoire as part of both *xianan* and *xiao liyuan* routes:

Lü Mengzheng 呂蒙正 was a narrative popular in the Yuan and Ming dynasties, often called *The Dilapidated Kiln* (*Poyao ji* 破窯記) or *The Painted Tower* (*Cailou ji* 彩樓記). Based on the biography of a tenth-century historical figure, the play involves an embroidered silk ball which the prime minister's daughter throws from a tower after having vowed that she will marry whomsoever it may hit. Though the man it strikes is only a poor scholar, she insists on keeping her vow. The scene in which she is taken to her new residence – 'Crossing the Bridge and Entering the Kiln' (Guoqiao ruyao 過橋入窯) – is a popular repertoire piece, alternating between comedy and pathos as the disappointed prime minister's daughter reaches, appraises and finally enters her squalid new residence.[16]

Xianan repertoire:

Su Qin 蘇秦 takes place in the Warring States and highlights the virtue of diligent application to learning. Despite his long years of devoted study, Su Qin is unable to reach high position, earning him and his wife the mockery and scorn of his family. When through perseverance he finally achieves high office, he first returns home in rags and is again mocked and attacked only to reveal himself as a high official. Ultimately he forgives his family despite the torments they have inflicted on him and especially his wife during their poverty.

Zheng Yuanhe, now commonly performed as *Li Yaxian.* That title stems from a 1957 adaptation by Lin Rensheng which took the script in a more literary direction. The story, derived from an eighth-century tale, has been widely popular for centuries in fiction and stage.[17] The concubine Li Yaxian saves Zheng Yuanhe from starvation and serves him as a virtuous wife, until Zheng becomes successful in the civil service examination, and the couple is rewarded.

Shanglu repertoire:

Cai Bojie 蔡伯喈 is the *liyuanxi* version of *The Lute* (*Pipa ji* 琵琶記) narrative. The story is enduringly popular across a range of *xiqu* theatres and has been much translated and adapted into other languages. Its presence on the recent *liyuanxi* stage, however, has only been sporadic. Shortly before her death in 1987, He Shumin gave an account of the choreography of 'Zhennü's Voyage' (Zhennü xing 真女行) to her student Wu Yihua 吳藝華, and was recorded singing and declaiming the lines from her hospital bed. Wu adapted these materials, and since that time has been the principal performer of this scene. In it, the heroine Zhao Zhennü 趙真女 (in other genres known as Zhao Wuniang 趙五娘) is left without news of her husband, who has left for the capital to sit the imperial examinations.[18] She takes to the road, playing the *pipa*, carrying a portrait she has piously made of her late parents-in-law. During the 1990s Su Yanshi, the troupe's vice director, revived another scene according to He's account, 'Entering the Niu Estate' (Ru Niu fu 入牛府), with Wu again in the role of the suffering heroine and Zeng Jingping playing the welcoming second wife, Niu Lihua 牛麗華. These were the only scenes from the narrative in repertoire until 2015, when the troupe decided to expand the story to fill an entire evening based on He's version in the *Collectanea*, billing it as a 'fragment' (*canben* 殘本).[19]

Liu Wenlong 劉文龍 is set in the Han dynasty. Liu, newly married, is captured by the Xiongnu, and returned to the Han only after twenty years. His wife, who has been pressured to remarry, has instead waited faithfully, leading to a finale in which loyalty and fidelity are rewarded. Perhaps by association with the theme of exile, this character is in other genres connected with Wang Zhaojun 王昭君 and Su Wu 蘇武, both Han figures compelled to live among the Xiongnu. However, the *liyuanxi* version, as given by He Shumin, does not mention either and probably reflects an earlier *nanxi* incarnation. A much longer Xuande script (1425–35), titled *The Golden Hairpin* (*Jinchai ji* 金釵記) excavated from a scholar's tomb near Chaozhou in 1975, gives context to the six scenes of He's oral account.[20]

Wang Kui 王魁 is a foundational *nanxi* script in which the student Wang Kui marries the courtesan Xie Guiying 謝桂英, vowing to temple gods that he will never betray her. However, once he has passed the exams, he makes a new and better match and ignores Guiying's desperate messages. Guiying kills herself in order to come back to haunt Wang Kui.[21] Unlike the many other versions in which Guiying wreaks her ghastly vengeance, in the *liyuanxi* practice Guiying's ghost is instead appeased by Wang Kui's promises that he will honour her with a memorial arch. The play was set down according to He Shumin's account, then rewritten for performance in the 1950s, despite the animus against ghost plays. Scholars have suggested, not least because Wang Kui is singularly unsympathetic to Guiying, that

84 LIYUANXI – CHINESE 'PEAR GARDEN THEATRE'

the *liyuanxi* version reflects an early *nanxi* plot.[22] A production drawing on the He text from the *Collectanea* was produced as part of the troupe's sixtieth anniversary celebrations in 2014.[23]

Wang Shipeng 王十朋 is a narrative known in later literati versions as *The Thorn Hairpin* (*Jingchai ji* 荆釵記). Although similar to the faithless scholar romance in structure – Wang Shipeng goes to the capital, where a marriage to the prime minister's daughter is proposed – in this case the scholar remains innocent and faithful, though a repudiation of his wife is manufactured by his powerful enemies.[24] In the end, both protagonists succeed in resisting the pressure to marry others and are happily reunited.

Zhu Shouchang 朱壽昌 is the dramatization of the life of an eleventh century official, held up as one of the *Twenty-four Filial Exemplars* (*Ershi si xiao* 二十四孝) for leaving his official position to search for his concubine mother.

The following section deals in greater detail with six important and popular pieces of current repertoire.

Traditional romantic play:
Chen San and Wuniang

From the very beginnings of what we now know as *liyuanxi*, the *Chen San and Wuniang* narrative occupies pride of place. A stele of 1566 – the same year as the first extant text of the narrative – attests to the story being widely disseminated in the Quanzhou and Zhangzhou areas by that time,[25] and the story also appears in numerous song books for *nanyin* troupes from roughly the same period.[26] Unlike most other *nanxi* stories, the characters and settings are clearly local, and there is no sign of the narrative being shared with or developed from the genres of central or northern China.

It has retained its centrality to repertoire. No narrative is more intimately associated with *liyuanxi* or indeed as tightly bound to Hokkien culture and identity as *Chen San and Wuniang*. It is a star-crossed love story which begins when a man of Quanzhou

Figure 3.1 *1954 performance of* Chen San and Wuniang, *with Su Wushui* 蘇烏水 *(c. 1931–2019) in the role of Wuniang and Su Ou* 蘇鷗 *(b. 1934) in the role of her maid, Yichun* 益春. *Both transitioned from being child actors before the revolution to becoming members of the state theatre in the early 1950s. Image by courtesy of the FPLET*

(Chen San) falls in love with a maiden of Chaozhou (Wuniang) at the Lantern Festival.[27] The FPLET troupe director Zeng describes it as 'the calling card of *liyuanxi*' and 'always sold out, no matter who is performing'. It enjoys widespread familiarity in the region: when performed in Quanzhou, certain arias are always

86   LIYUANXI – CHINESE 'PEAR GARDEN THEATRE'

supplemented by humming from members of the audience. It was with this play that *liyuanxi* captured national attention (1954; Fig. 3.1) and that generated the first (and only extant) *liyuanxi* feature film (1956).[28] In recent decades, *Chen San and Wuniang* has also been the most frequent choice for performance during the visit of various Hokkien theatres to the diaspora and further afield, and Wuniang's long solo scenes of wistful longing such as 'Great Melancholy' have produced some of *liyuanxi*'s greatest successes on the national and the international stage.

Today, every year's Lantern Festival season in Quanzhou ends with a version of the narrative extended over three nights, although historically the play might have lasted for nine.[29] Besides *liyuanxi*, the narrative is in repertoire throughout the genres of the Hokkien-speaking region (*nanyin*, puppet genres, *gezaixi*) as well as in the Chaozhou (Teochew) cultural area's own theatre of *chaoju* 潮劇. In print and stage versions it also has a considerable history in Southeast Asia, and indeed, it is possible that the narrative – with its boundary-crossing between the provinces of Fujian and Guangdong and the star-crossed wandering between the cultural areas of Quanzhou and Chaozhou – had a particular resonance for Hokkien and Teochew migrants.[30] Known in the Dutch East Indies by its Hokkien pronunciation, *Tan Sha Go Nio*, a translation was published in Malay in Semarang in 1886, adapted or translated by Boen Sing Hoo, and reprinted twice.[31] Five more versions in prose and verse were published between 1902 and 1930, and it is more than likely that it was staged there throughout this period in various performance genres.[32]

Although the plot features many convolutions, its basic contours are simple. Visiting his brother, the Quanzhou man Chen San has stopped in Chaozhou, where he falls in love at first sight with Wuniang. Unfortunately, a local tyrant's son sees her on the same evening and tries to arrange to wed her. Attracted by the prospect of a rich marriage, Wuniang's father agrees to the match. Chen returns to Chaozhou to look for her, and Wuniang sees him mounted on his white horse. Wuniang drops entwined lychees from her balcony to symbolize her attachment to him. Now assured that his affections are returned, Chen San comes disguised as a journeyman worker to work in her father's home. When he deliberately breaks a valuable mirror, he becomes a bondservant, ostensibly to pay off the debt he has incurred, but actually so that he can be close to Wuniang and orchestrate opportunities to be alone with her. Wuniang, who guesses his scheme, is torn between acquiescing and resisting his overtures. Unable to overcome her reticence, Chen San decides to depart for Quanzhou, leaving a letter which so moves Wuniang that she agrees to run away with him. They elope and are married there. The latter part of the narrative concerns how Chen San, with the help of his brother, succeeds in making his marriage accepted.

The adaptation, written by Lin Rensheng and others, was based on Cai Youben's recollections and written for the Eastern China Opera Observation and Performance Convention in Shanghai in 1954.[33] This reduction of *Chen San and Wuniang* to a single-evening version was intended to make the repertoire 'performable', as the vocabulary of the day put it. In his account of his adaptation of *Chen San*, Lin's attention to cleaning up the narrative for political purposes is evident:

> this play has, under the great leadership of the party and the government, undergone six rather substantial revisions. The first version was in the summer of the 1952. It was derived from the thirty-plus scenes originally narrated by the elder artist Cai Youben as well as the scene 'Admiring Flowers' as narrated by the elder artist Xu Zhiren 許志仁, and the 51-scene woodcut script *Lizhi ji* 荔枝記. We removed the rubbish in the second half where Chen San has to depend on his brother's feudal influence to secure marriage.[34]

This concern about 'feudal influence' cut out not only the last third of the play and the original beginning, but also all the coarse and more suggestive parts.[35]

While the single-session version has become standard in the years since *Chen San and Wuniang* was revived, it has also undergone further change. Beginning in 1997, one scene 'Sweeping the Floor' (Saodi 掃地) has typically been removed to keep the performance within a certain length. However, a 2002 performance in Taiwan, staged over three days, provided an opportunity to incorporate other elements of the repertoire that were dormant (those known to older actors or learned at school though later not performed).

The narrative's foundational position in repertoire and technique has also made it an integral part of education and thus a convenient way to stage 'transmission'. In 2014, as the troupe celebrated its sixtieth anniversary,[36] the play again closed the festival on Lantern Festival eve; as a special display of transmission, six different actors from six different acting generations (entering the troupe in 1956, 1957, 1960, 1977, 1997 and 2007) performed the roles of Chen San and Wuniang, the oldest performer being over seventy and the youngest under twenty.[37]

Traditional ghost play:
Zhu Wen and the Lucky Coins

Zhu Wen and the Lucky Coins (*Zhu Wen Taiping qian* 朱文太平錢) is not among the most frequently performed of *liyuanxi* plays, but it occupies an important place in repertoire as a rare, old and distinctive narrative. Its title is recorded in the early fifteenth-century *Yongle Compendium* and other Ming texts, but only fragments from the period survive. Two scenes survive in *Mantian chun* as does a longer incomplete version from the Daoguang period (1821–50). Its recovery in 1953 as part of the new state theatre's efforts to gather historic texts represented an important step to situating the genre in Chinese theatre history, and show a substantive and unique link to *nanxi*.[38]

The plot concerns the scholar Zhu Wen, who, as he travels to take part in the imperial examinations, meets and is seduced by a girl, A Grain of Gold (Yilijin 一 粒金, in some texts Yinianjin 一 捻金). Having presented him with the gift of a casket, she arranges a rendezvous with him. When Zhu arrives at the inn where he is to meet her, the innkeeping couple tell him that the casket belongs to the innkeeper's late adoptive daughter. Shown her portrait, Zhu Wen absconds in terror, but in a following scene the ghost convinces him that she is at least human enough for their romance to be without danger. A final scene is known to have existed, but how the drama ended is uncertain.

In shadow play versions, and perhaps in the ur-version, there is a much more complex story involving not only a ghost but several other supernatural figures.[39] The title of the *nanxi* version, *Zhu Wen Flees the Ghost* (*Zhu Wen zou gui* 朱文走鬼), certainly indicates supernatural interventions, but in the 1950s stage performing ghost plays could be problematic and the FPLET would not have wished to be accused of superstition. Thus, in that version, the male lead is proletarianized, the woman is clearly a human and the ghost plot merely a story invented by her adoptive parents.[40] Completed and adapted by Lin Rensheng, its 1955 performances in Beijing were a further key to the genre's revival. Lin's more fundamental interventions – initially motivated by the pressures of the *xiqu* reform era – were reversed in a 1960 version, and the full Daoguang era script was published in 1991.[41] The three-scene version performed today incorporates materials from the traditional and the post-1949 script, and is now often understood as telling a story of love triumphing over death.

Its 1955 success in Beijing, following hard upon the text's rediscovery and the 1954 triumph of *Chen San and Wuniang*, did much to secure the troupe's place in the PRC's *xiqu* hierarchy and the genre's connection with southern drama. Since then, the play has often been revived, in part to buttress the genre's claims to being the inheritor of *nanxi*. The role of A Grain of Gold in 1987 also marked the emergence of Zeng Jingping as a leading performer of the genre, capable of combining her own innovations within traditional frameworks.

Traditional humorous play:
Zhu Maichen

Zhu Maichen is both an old and a familiar narrative in the Chinese theatre world.[42] As one scholar has noted, 'we know that more or less since the beginning of Chinese drama, [Zhu Maichen's] personal life has been staged, generation after generation; and, one supposes as long as there is drama in China, they will continue to perform Zhu Maichen divorcing his wife'.[43] It is also an unusual story, since it tells the story of a woman who, over two thousand years ago, demands and receives a divorce. Historically and in most genres the narrative usually illustrates the punishment meted out to a woman who is disloyal to her husband, but various twentieth-century authors adapted the story to question or lament the patriarchy, and even in traditional productions actresses have often taken a more interrogative approach and used the plight of Zhu Maichen's wife to reconsider the situation of women in traditional China.

However, the narrative has not always received the grim and righteous treatment. As early as the Yuan dynasty there were also versions with happy endings, where divorce ends not in the wife's suicide but in the couple's happy reunion. In one *zaju* version, in the tradition of virtuous wives (and reminiscent of other such *liyuanxi* pieces as Li Yaxian 李亞仙), Zhu Maichen's wife is perturbed by the effect that her proximity has on her husband's studiousness, and forces him to grant her a divorce in order to remove distractions and compel him to prepare for his exams. Once he has triumphed and obtained a high administrative position, the evidence of her collusion is adduced and a happy ending eventuates.[44]

Liyuanxi's version, too, produces what might be called a happy ending, although the mechanisms to produce it are rather different. As with much of the rest of traditional *liyuanxi* repertoire, there is reason for supposing that this may reflect an older *nanxi* legacy, but only a small portion of the narrative survived to be written down in the mid-twentieth century.[45] Categorized as *shanglu* repertoire, in the post-Cultural Revolution era two scenes have been in repertoire: 'Forced to Write the Divorce Document' (Bixie 逼寫) and 'Entrusting Remarriage to Zhang Gong' (Tuogong 托公), both well known as 'talking scenes' (*zuibaixi* 嘴白戲) repertoire, where the theatricality emerges more from comical repartee than from singing.[46] A 1956 transcript, for the most part dictated by the troupe's most prominent female performer, He Shumin, is included in the *Collectanea*.[47] For a 2016 revival, this text was supplemented by the fragmentary memories of older actors regarding other scenes, either from performance or from education as child or adolescent actors. With the assistance of retired elder performers (most notably Cai Qingping 蔡清平 consulting on how to perform the title role), a six-scene revival was established and has been in repertoire since.

That 2016 revival has been part of a twenty-first-century FPLET initiative to revive older plays in their fragmentary 'original forms', largely drawing on the *Collectanea*. Zeng Jingping may also have been drawn to the play for the opportunity it presents for her to act against type, since she usually performs elegant maidens and widows, rather than a shrewish character such as Zhu Maichen's wife. The fact that these scenes in *liyuanxi* practice are fragments means that the modern production occurs in narrative sequence, but without regard for narrative proportion: the pacing of the narrative is determined not by an overarching logic of a script, but by the happenstance of a performance practice which has retained some scenes (which narratively might be of an aleatory nature) and not others (which might be more central to the plot). Since, however, the audience generally knows the whole plot anyway, they can supply the missing or underdeveloped parts of the narrative.

At over three hours, the full version of this 'fragment' is deemed too long for some audiences, and so amendments of the show mean that this version has also been performed with

92 LIYUANXI – CHINESE 'PEAR GARDEN THEATRE'

five scenes and other abridgments. Prominent performances were given at the 2016 Shanghai Little Theatre Chinese Opera Festival and in November 2017 alongside *The Imperial Stele* in Beijing as the 'When Love Is Gone' (Dang ai yicheng wangshi 當愛已成往事) series. The production was capped by a performance at the Hong Kong Chinese Opera Festival in June 2019, and also included shows in Nanjing and the Zhejiang cities of Ningbo and Jinhua.

The first scene, 'Bixie', involves the attempts made by Zhao Xiaoniang – fed up with years of poverty – to force her husband Zhu Maichen to sign a document of divorce. In the *liyuanxi* version, there is little opportunity for the pathos and sense of tremendous moment this scene often produces in genres such as *kunqu* – the high drama of a woman taking a step that the audience knows she will wish to recant. Instead, it is the scrappy humour of the bickering couple which predominates, added to the spectacle of the henpecked husband. The wife is brash, demanding, crude and curt; as soon as she appears it is to berate and insult her husband. When Zhu Maichen's friend, Zhang Gong, tries to intervene on her husband's side, Zhao replies:

> I, Zhao Xiaoniang, have never quarrelled with anyone and lost. If I were defeated by you, Zhang-Gong-from-the-neighbouring-village, it would really make me sick. You are no family of [Zhu Maichen], no relative, not even a distant uncle.[48]

The invective is accompanied by physical comedy: for instance, in the process of being bullied into agreeing to divorce, Zhu Maichen asks for brush and paper to write the divorce document – and she instantly produces them from within her costume, showing that she is ready to divorce at any moment. During the first scene, Zhao bumps into her aunt, who is acting as her matchmaker for a second and more prosperous marriage. As they back into each other, Zhao says, 'I've run into a poxy sow', and the aunt remarks that 'I've run into a dog', leading into coarse and punning banter between the two of them. Since the two women share the same goal – to have Zhao remarried – the exchange does little for the plot but serves the purpose of amusing the audience and defining the two female characters as stroppy and greedy.

In another scene, the prospective bridegroom for the remarriage is produced: a pathetically comical figure with a limp, a stutter and a limited intelligence focused on food. He laments that the wedding will be broken off, with loss of promised delights: the celebratory pork knuckle has already been stewed. Comically, he bemoans the disappearance of his 'pork knuckle wife'. Such banter, grotesque, convoluted and dialect-bound, is a constant feature of the play, and is underscored with slapstick physical comedy.

The play reaches a happy ending when Zhu agrees to take his old wife back, though (presumably as a vestige of the moral punishment) she will be subordinate to his new wife. The scene ends with more slightly risqué repartee, this time between Zhu Maichen's new mother-in-law, Madam Ni, and Zhao Xiaoniang, and in which they discuss how Zhu should be divided among his two wives:

Madam Ni From the crown of the head to the chest, this is one part.

Xiaoniang Who's that for?

Madam Ni That part is for my daughter. To talk about love at night. I'll cut you up too, woman!

Xiaoniang I don't think you would.

Madam Ni You want a part of him too, woman?

Xiaoniang Which part is for me?

Madam Ni Well, everyone gets a part. You get a part too. From the toe up to the thigh ...

94   LIYUANXI – CHINESE 'PEAR GARDEN THEATRE'

Xiaoniang Who's that part for?

Madam Ni This part is for you, woman, so you can sniff his foot in the dark.

So, rather than the pathos, the *liyuanxi* version operates as a popular comedy, with the titular Zhu Maichen merely a background figure for the travails of Xiaoniang. With the match off, Zhao becomes not a miserably remarried wife, whose claim to be taken back by Zhu Maichen is socially impossible, but a single divorcee who can be recovered for respectability through repentance. This grants her bitterness and remorse a different tinge because she has given up her marriage not for a worse one, but for nothing at all. Instead, she is reduced to sweeping the streets. Even here, her self-pity and snappishness are deployed not to produce empathy but laughter. The crucial element that permits the happy end way is that Xiaoniang's second wedding does not come off, and so her connubial chastity is not really impugned, despite her efforts to find a new husband. With the shrewishness of the wife deployed to comic effect, moral admonition is clothed in mirth. As Zeng Jingping explained about this role, 'it requires you to get hold of the proper degree. Once, because the audience was into it, I overdid it, and then she wasn't adorable anymore. She has to be shrewish enough to be funny, but not so shrewish that people don't pity her later on'.[49]

Ultimately, the effect of a comical treatment of this story – by all appearances a treatment that has historical roots – is in fact *more* rather than less conservative, as indeed one might expect of southern Fujian's theatre culture, which tended, if the 1950s *Collectanea* is to be believed, to reproduce neo-Confucian mores until the Communist Revolution. The integrity of marriage is no longer really threatened. Secondary female characters (ridiculous aunt, matchmaker, mother-in-law) are all greedy and preposterous, and the happy return of Xiaoniang (as a subordinate wife) is secured by the magnanimity of Zhu Maichen but also of the neighbour, Zhang Gong, who intercedes on her behalf. Female demands for a better life are, in this version, a matter to put off as the subject of farce. Ultimately, this dismissal of Zhu Maichen's wife is even less sympathetic to the aspirations of a woman unhappy in her marriage. This patriarchal strain of the repertoire does much to explain why post-Mao scripts, with their sympathetic focus on the plight of women in traditional society, have proven so pathbreaking.

Contemporary tragic play: *The Chaste Woman's Lament*

The Chaste Woman's Lament (1987; revised 2006) is derived from an episode titled 'The Two Fingers Commendation' (Liangzhi tijing 兩指題旌) in *Humorous Notes from an Ancient Bell* (*Xie duo* 諧鐸) by Qing literatus and dramatist Shen Qifeng 沈起鳳 (1741–1802). The source text is only a brief passage, situated in a collection of strange or comical tales. It relates how a woman, ashamed at her unchaste behaviour, cuts off her fingers to remind herself of her trespasses. When many years later her son achieves high office through the examination system, she is honoured for her self-admonition.[50]

The script was playwright Wang Renjie's first national success and was awarded the 1986–7 Cao Yu Dramatic Literature Prize (Cao Yu xiju wenxue jiang 曹禺戲劇文學獎).[51] The play and production won great esteem in theatre circles, with the Taiwanese playwright Wang An-chi 王安祈 (b. 1955) adapting it for the *jingju* stage in 1990 as *Ask the Heavens* (*Wen tian* 問天).[52]

Wang Renjie's account of how he came to use this material is typically nonchalant:

At the time, the troupe was waiting for a script to participate in the summer performance series, I was sweating bullets, and it seemed best just to take the story of 'The Two Fingers

Commendation' (only a few hundred characters long), with its pretty young widow, and its dissolute scholar, so I cudgelled my brains and racked my poor wit, in the hopes of turning this into a play, one that would be an authentic *liyuanxi* play.[53]

The plot concerns a young and beautiful widow, Madam Yan 顏氏, who has taken a young scholar, Shen Rong 沈蓉, into her employ as tutor for her son. Shen is preparing to go

Figure 3.2 *Programme of* The Chaste Woman's Lament *for 1988 performances in Beijing, designed by Wang Renjie's good friend, the Quanzhou artist and calligrapher Lin Jianpu* 林劍僕. *Image by courtesy of the FPLET*

REPERTOIRE 97

to the capital to sit for exams, but Madam Yan – smitten by his studiousness and literary talent – extracts from him a promise to return after the examinations, whether or not he passes. In apostrophes, both acknowledge attraction, but Shen is intent on his prospects of high official career, and regards his inclination toward her as at worst a trap and at best a fallback should his prospects dim.

That same night, after much soul-searching, Madam Yan calls on him in his quarters, ostensibly to give him money to defray his travel costs for his journey to the capital. Her visit is conspicuous by its late hour and the feebleness of her pretext, and when she attempts further advances, Shen overcomes temptation and coldly rejects her. When her renewed attempts are rebuffed, she flees in humiliation and despair. Eager to shut her out once and for all, Shen hastily tries to shut himself in, but catches her fingers in the door just as she turns back to re-enter the room. She runs away in pain and misery. Alone and in desperate pain, she cuts off her fingers as a way of reminding herself of her shameful behaviour, and as a reminder that her responsibility is only to her son, whom henceforth she must foster in his studies as a virtuous mother ought.

When, sixteen years later, her son passes the highest degree and becomes a high official, Shen Rong sees an opportunity to present himself in a positive light. He writes to the emperor telling him of Madam Yan's devotion, which he commends, not incidentally highlighting his own triumph over temptation. The emperor, amused by the story, grants her a high but ambiguous honour: she is to be publicly praised for being 'tardily chaste'. Rather than honoured, Madam Yan feels humiliated by the way that her son's triumph has nonetheless redounded to her shame. She hangs herself. Wang's revised version of 2006 gave her a somewhat more ambiguous ending, in that she exits, and vowing to 'quietly sing the chaste woman's lament'.[54]

The Chaste Woman's Lament transformed an anecdote intended as humorous (and still callously interpreted in the play by the emperor as a good laugh) into a tragic struggle against inexorable fate. The misogynistic vein that the humorous anecdote depends on has been replaced by a bitter critique of the lack of agency for widows trapped in expectations of chastity. This forms part of Wang's career-long concern with questions surrounding the status of women. Having wagered everything for a chance at romance and perhaps respectable love, the agony of rejection gives rise to Madam Yan's decision to mutilate herself to remind her of (and ensure) her chastity in future. But even that sacrifice is only temporarily successful, since – even as she celebrates her son's examination glory – masculine vanity again disturbs her peace of mind, when Shen Rong chooses to callously lay her transgression bare. Madam Yan's momentary expression of desire results in an unextinguishable shame, even as the state and the patriarchy cloak that shame in official honour. Along with *Scholar Dong and Madam Li*, the play must also be understood within the context of China's increasing acceptance of female agency – including female desire, divorce and remarriage – during the late 1980s and the 1990s.[55]

An enduring concern in modern Chinese literature has been the question of what works meet a definition of tragedy (and whether such a term is useful in the Chinese context). This question developed under the influence of one strain of the Western philosophical tradition which posited that tragedy was the highest of the literary arts.[56] Although based on a late imperial source and performed according to *liyuanxi* tradition, the basic structure of *The Chaste Woman's Lament* – in which a woman, despite all her efforts to struggle against fate, is crushed by an inexorable mechanism that is traced back to a single misstep – suggests the influence of the Western classical tragedy. While attempts to scour the classical canon for examples of tragedy have not always proven convincing, Wang's drama may be classed as a successful modern tragic drama, the conditions of grinding, inescapable fate being provided by a modern retrospective on the status of women in imperial China.

Contemporary humorous play: *Scholar Dong and Madam Li*

Scholar Dong and Madam Li has been the FPLET's greatest success in the post-Mao years, and its place in the troupe's history is comparable only to the 1954 debut of the genre on the national stage with *Chen San and Wuniang*. *Scholar Dong* is in several ways an unusual script. Once again, Wang's approach was highly innovative, taking the usually sombre themes of the fate of widows in China's (unspecified) imperial past and treating them with playfulness and irreverence, sometimes of a rather lusty variety. Much admired nationally, the play has been adapted several times into other genres of *xiqu* throughout the country, but FPLET's version production remains the best-known, and has remained in repertoire since its premiere. *Scholar Dong and Madam Li* begins with the mortal illness of Councillor Peng, who – on the point of being carried off to the underworld by ghosts – summons his friend,

Figure 3.3 *Scholar Dong (Gong Wanli* 龔萬里*) and Madam Li (Zeng Jingping) celebrate the triumph of love at the conclusion of* Scholar Dong and Madam Li. *Image by courtesy of the FPLET*

100   LIYUANXI – CHINESE 'PEAR GARDEN THEATRE'

the unmarried scholar Dong Siwei, to his bedside. Peng instructs Dong that after his own death, Dong is to be responsible for the chastity of Madam Li, Peng's wife. Dong, financially indebted to Peng, has no choice but to comply with the wishes of the dying man, who in return forgives the loan by destroying the documentation. Peng is carried off to the underworld, satisfied that he has secured his widow's chastity; Madam Li is neither consulted nor informed about the arrangement.

Dong's awkward guardianship puts him constantly in the widow's way and exposes him to the mockery of his tutees and Madam Li's servants. Piqued by the surveillance, Madam Li fans his suspicions rather than seeking to defuse them. Dong, increasingly convinced that she is indulging in illicit trysts, is blind to his own increasing infatuation with her charms. Obsessed with finding her *in flagrante delicto*, he finally climbs the wall that divides their residences and bursts into her chambers on the suspicion of her infidelity. He finds her alone – or, rather, she declares coyly, *he* is the only man present. Overcoming his scruples and his dread of the dead Councillor Peng, Dong follows her into the bedchamber.

The following day is one of reckoning, when Dong must make his report about Madam Li's behaviour at Councillor Peng's grave. The ghost, who appears as a disembodied voice, already knows about the transgressions and shouts down Dong's feeble protestations. He demands that Dong put the unchaste widow to death. She is willing to submit to this punishment, and it seems for a moment that their transgression will be gruesomely punished. Instead, in one of the most astonishing moments of contemporary Chinese drama, Dong ratchets up his courage to confront the ghost on moral grounds. What right do the dead have to trample on the happiness of the living? Instead of carrying out the designated punishment, Dong instead threatens to disinter Peng from his tomb, whereupon the ghost fearfully acquiesces and scuttles off in confusion. Love triumphs.

Premiered in 1993, commentators and audience members saw in the plot a rejection of older social narratives of female subservience in favour of feminine agency and sexual liberty. The cruelties of the past would no longer dictate the lives of the present. Whereas in *The Chaste Woman's Lament*, social order proves implacable – and in the name of chastity exacts a cruel price – in *Scholar Dong*, conventions and received morality are subverted, even overthrown. The traditional social and gender order, rewritten for a contemporary audience's benefit, cannot rule from beyond the tomb, and mature single people are allowed to arrange their lives without reference to the dead or to hostile institutions. This can be read as expanding the modern rejection of arranged marriages and traditional mores in order to embrace also the freedoms of the widowed or divorced. Taking the allegory into political territory, the central premise can even suggest a post-Mao reconsideration of the high political pieties of the preceding era. As Wang remarked to a French journalist, 'It's very convenient to use the past to satirize the present, and it makes people laugh … It's all about knowing how far you can go. It's like ping-pong: the ball has to hit the table right at the edge'.[57]

In some ways, the play seems like an obverse of *The Chaste Woman's Lament*. It shares with the earlier work a plot concerning a widow who has conceived a desire for an unattached man in her vicinity, with *Scholar Dong* retaining the question of the lives of women in premodern Chinese society and composing it in a sunnier, comical key. The interest of both stories also coincides in that the match is eligible in modern audience terms, but is illicit in terms of traditional morality. The characters must navigate the disgrace this desire generates, triumphing over it in *Scholar Dong* but with tragic consequences in *Lament*. The parallels between the two plays did not go unnoticed in PRC drama studies, with one scholar considering Madam Yan on the one hand to 'tear away the ugly face of male chauvinism' and Madam Li to represent 'a projection of glorious idealism'.[58] In a long historical view, *Scholar Dong* is perhaps the more traditional (though less historically plausible) treatment, since a happy ending is characteristic of traditional repertoire.

The play quickly achieved national success after its premiere at the 19th Fujian Drama Festival in October 1993. In 1994, the script was published in *Juben* (drama scripts) alongside an admiring analysis by Qu Liuyi 曲六乙 (b. 1930), an important establishment arbiter of official and academic *xiqu* taste. The play was performed in Beijing (1998) and in Taiwan (2000) and Hong Kong (2001). In 2003, the production was retooled under the direction of Lu Ang 盧昂 of the Shanghai Dramatic Conservatory, and with these changes was eligible for selection in the National Stage Arts Masterpieces Project (Guojia wutai yishu jingpin gongcheng 國家舞台藝術精品工程). In 2008 the show was performed as part of the artistic programme of the Beijing Olympics, and in 2013 it received the Grand Prize for Outstanding Repertory Piece and toured nationally again.

Revising for gender:
The Imperial Stele

The Imperial Stele takes us to the question of gender and generation in *xiqu* playwrighting. *Xiqu* drama as a category of literary production remains more male-dominated than other genres, such as fiction, poetry, essays and spoken drama. Though there are perhaps two dozen known female authors of theatre in the late imperial era, the earliest of whom wrote in the mid-seventeenth century, none of them is canonical.[59]

Gender balance in *xiqu* writing has improved only slightly in modern times, and plays by women are skewed to those genres where women predominate onstage and in administrative roles. For instance, several female playwrights of the Jiangnan *yueju* form have been women, a fact surely related to the fact that it is a female-dominated (and these days, -managed) genre. The balance seems somewhat more even in Taiwan, where one of the most prominent *xiqu* dramatists (and academics) is Wang An-chi, who has also been deeply committed to making *jingju* relevant for young Taiwanese audiences.

Zhang Jingjing 張婧婧 (b. 1987) in 2009 became the first female playwright in the *liyuanxi* tradition. The fact that she is also from outside the region – a Nanjinger, she came to *xiqu* as a devoted fan of the national prestige genre, *kunqu* – is a sign that *liyuanxi* is increasingly part of the give and take of national *xiqu* culture. Zhang's concerns with female desire and the legitimacy and feasibility of its expression in a patriarchal society echo themes Wang Renjie had introduced in *The Chaste Woman's Lament* and *Scholar Dong*. In 2015, her script *The Imperial Stele* became the first *liyuanxi* work by a woman to be produced; indeed, *The Imperial Stele* also features women as principal performer, central character, stage director and playwright. The script was published in *Fujian Yishu*, and it has won several provincial prizes since its 2015 premiere, and entered regular repertoire.

As with Wang Renjie's plays, there is a late imperial source, in this case a play that remains well known in *jingju* repertoire. As performed traditionally, the plot of *The Imperial Stele* can appear misogynistic. In that and related versions, the talented scholar Wang Youdao 王有道 sets off to sit the imperial exams, leaving his young wife Meng Yuehua 孟月華 alone with his sister. Her parents send for Meng, requesting that she stay with them over the Qing Ming festival in order to join their annual excursion to sweep the ancestral graves. She obeys. However, concerned for her sister-in-law, who is alone at home, Meng returns to check on her. Surprised en route by a rain shower, she takes refuge in a small pavilion containing an imperial stele, where she resigns herself to wait the storm out. But the rain continues.

As dusk falls, a young scholar, Liu Shengchun 柳生春, also shelters from the storm in this Imperial Stele Pavilion. The two are forced to share the same small space all night, to their mutual discomfort. Theatrically speaking, the core of the play is generated by the tension between the two characters' proximity, acutely conscious of one another's presence but unwilling to speak to each other in order not to offend propriety. Liu occupies himself with virtuous reading,

104   LIYUANXI – CHINESE 'PEAR GARDEN THEATRE'

while Meng sings anxious soliloquies, her concerns somewhat allayed as she recognizes that the cultivated stranger means her no harm and that they are equally embarrassed; meanwhile, they both count the hours until day breaks and they can each hasten home. Meng is met by her sister-in-law, who is alarmed by her bedraggled state.

Soon thereafter, Wang Youdao returns from his exams to find his wife sick in bed from the chill she has caught on the fateful night; Wang's sister reluctantly gives him an account of what has happened in his absence. Although the sister lays special emphasis on Meng's chaste behaviour, Wang is irate and divorces her for perceived immorality. For Wang, he needs no further proof of guilt than that she has been alone with a strange man overnight, and he banishes her from their home. Meng leaves in great distress.

Before long, the imperial examiner summons Wang Youdao and Liu Shengchun, who have both passed the metropolitan exams. The examiner has been supernaturally advised of Liu's special moral feats (his paper, discarded by the examiner, repeatedly and magically reappears at the top of the sheaf of exams). After some prodding, he elicits from Liu the story of the night spent chastely in the pavilion with Meng. Putting two and two together, Wang realizes that Liu's account exactly matches that of his wife, and that she indeed acted with all due propriety on the fateful night. The examiner congratulates Wang on the virtue of his wife. But, finding out that the suspicious husband has divorced her, he admonishes Wang urgently to find her and plead for her to forgive him. Wang rushes to her parents' house and kneels before her in contrition, at which point she takes him back to the satisfaction of all.

Unsurprisingly, this plot has proven unsatisfactory, even risible, for many young women, including Zhang. Her rewriting – which has the effect of rehabilitating a story that now appears patriarchal if not misogynistic – can be considered experimental insofar as it changes the mechanics of the plot, but it is careful not to disturb the boundaries of the genre.[60] Of course, gender relations and gender representation throughout *xiqu* (and indeed the classical heritage as a whole) present challenges for contemporary audiences and readers, from the blaming of women for political disaster (e.g. the Tang Minghuang and Yang Guifei narrative) and the approval of the murder of women for infidelity (e.g. the Yan Poxi and Song Jiang narrative) to the vilification of women for initiating divorce (the Zhu Maichen's wife narrative). Zhang's work is thus to be situated in a century of adaptation (often through spoken dramas) to critique and recover misogynistic repertoire.

Zhang's interventions in the plot of *The Imperial Stele* are substantial, but the same three characters remain at the script's core. Meng Yuehua is a young wife whose husband Wang Youdao leaves for the capital. While he is away, she is still caught in a rainstorm and forced to retire to the pavilion, where the scholar shortly also arrives, a circumstance which provokes the divorce; Wang is still moved to rescind his hasty act when he realizes his wife's virtue. In Zhang's version, however, the characters of Meng's parents and of Wang's sister are removed; the plot is restricted to the two scholars and Meng. There is thus a dramatic zeroing in on the psychology of the three characters, combined with a greater backstory. Wang shows from the beginning of the play a disinclination to be interested in his wife rather than his studies; the scene is thus prepared for her to reject him on grounds not only of jealousy but also of neglect and egotism. Wang discovers that Meng has spent the night in the pavilion because he finds a telling poem she has written about that night. When he begins to doubt her fidelity, she is offended and writes the divorce papers herself, leaving of her own volition and filled with righteous wrath rather than shame and humility. Most strikingly, when instructed to go fetch and forgive his wife, both scholars go to the pavilion, but they find Meng sceptical of both their friendly overtures. It is not entirely clear, as the play ends, whether she will return home or not; or perhaps even leave with the scholar. Instead, Meng Yuehua strides into the distance, having asserted her right to self-determination.[61]

In conversation, Zhang suggested that her rewriting was not meant to repudiate traditional standards of feminine virtue, which at some level she respects, but rather the way Meng's life is situated within a structure where her account can receive no credence and actions taken against her cannot be redressed. Zhang asks, 'Is it fixed that women's emotions and self-respect have to be ignored or betrayed in this way?' Her issue with the traditional *jingju* version was that it was a 'psychological illustration' that failed to fill in crucial information. For instance: 'What is the marriage between Wang Youdao and Meng Yuehua like, does Wang Youdao love her? What about Meng Yuehua's feelings for Wang Youdao?' Nor did it seem possible that left alone in the pavilion, the thoughts of Meng would revolve only around virtue, or that when Wang Youdao asks for forgiveness, she happily returns to him without reservation. The logic of the play struck Zhang as being 'impeded'. Thus, her rewriting can be seen as an attempt to introduce psychological realism from a woman's perspective.

Zhang's oeuvre since that time has similarly been concerned with gender, including her 2017 sophomore effort *Li Shishi* 李師師, in which Zhang rewrote the fall of the Song from the perspective not of the last emperor, Huizong, but telling the story instead as revolving around his beloved concubine, whose strength of mind stands in contrast to the emperor's indecisiveness. There is thus considerable hope that Zhang and other young female playwrights will continue to constructively critique and recreate traditional repertoire by means of adaptation.

Conclusions

Within and outside of China, a focus on the largest cities and the centres of economic and political power distorts the country's image, not least in the realm of culture. The result in the field of theatre is an inordinate focus on urban spoken theatre as well as on the putatively 'national' or 'classical' *xiqu* genres of *jingju* and *kunqu*, with the rest of the country relegated to being 'local' or 'regional'. This hierarchy is one expression of a more general and an increasing tendency to define the nation in terms of a singular, national, Mandarin-speaking culture, with the rich tapestry of other forms being reduced to the folkloric.

Since 'national' genres have also been the focus of revolution and reform, however, it has sometimes been advantageous to a genre like *liyuanxi* to be at a certain remove. As the leading theatre critic Fu Jin 傅謹 (b. 1956) writes, though the historic prosperity of Quanzhou was important for the development of *liyuanxi*, it is also paradoxically serendipitous for this tradition that in the more recent past the region has been peripheral, since 'in cultural terms it has not been much attacked and destroyed – only in this way could a dash of Chinese culture's highest glory, even as it vanishes, have been transmitted here intact into the present'.[1]

This brief introductory volume is in some degree an account of the survival of one classical theatre into the contemporary period, against considerable odds. The tradition of theatre in

108   LIYUANXI – CHINESE 'PEAR GARDEN THEATRE'

southern Fujian is one of the longest and most vibrant in China, and *liyuanxi* is its most distinct and most literary expression. Centred on a city which is home to a fiercely proud, local and transnational culture, *liyuanxi* attracts profound admiration within its cultural sphere, even if intra-Chinese cultural and linguistic barriers have limited its appreciation domestically. As a theatre genre performed by a single professional troupe, *liyuanxi* must contend with a restricted infrastructure and heightened risks – since practices altered or repertoire retired will not be retained elsewhere. On the other hand, there is prestige, pride and a sense of historic responsibility associated with the circumstance that a single troupe is the sole interpreter of the form.

Xiqu genres must contend with the double-edged sword of 'tradition'. The cultural historian Joshua Goldstein, writing about the Republican era, noted that *xiqu* faced 'the teleological assumptions which lie at the heart of ideological construction of a colonial modernity – that the modern involves dynamic change as opposed to the stasis of tradition',[2] and this observation is still true today. *Liyuanxi* has in the post-Mao era demonstrated the viability of *xiqu* as a contemporary art as much as any other genre. It has revived and maintained tradition while producing new scripts that have again and again demonstrated contemporary relevance, be it in the approach to questions of gender order, sexual morality, local identity or self-determination, all within the boundaries of a classical art form.

At the same time, all contemporary performances contain substantial and ongoing adaptation or creation in all aspects and inherit over the course of several periods, even as pressure to represent genres like *liyuanxi* as 'classical' limits the extent to which contemporary processes can be acknowledged. Recognizing the heritage of genres like *liyuanxi*, valorizing their practice as living theatres and accepting their artistry as mining rather than curating (let alone reproducing) a substantial tradition can help free *xiqu* from its image as a static, technique-limited theatre. While the nature of older *xiqu* forms regulates many

CONCLUSIONS 109

aspects of performance, including physical technique, costuming and make-up, there is no reason to regard these restrictions as inherently anti-modern or unchanging. The persistent image of these arts as inherited 'merely' tradition-bound is inappropriate. Since the materials on which performances draw are both narratively and technically traditional, tradition is revealed not as a limitation but instead as the indispensable resource of *xiqu*.

In countless ways – including stage dimensions, costume styles and materials, performance length and context, ritual importance, patronage system and audience composition, sociopolitical context, actor training and social class, make-up ingredients, ticketing – there can be no doubt of drastic, unavoidable and constant change. Ashley Thorpe's observations that *jingju* ('Peking opera') 'has been constantly reformed and altered' and that 'defining Jingju as a singular set of practices has always been problematic'[3] can be extended to any genre of *xiqu*, including *liyuanxi*. The dance scholar Emily Wilcox's recent formulation of tradition in China as a 'dynamic inheritance', both evolving and grounded in a specific set of techniques and principles, applies equally to *xiqu* genres such as *liyuanxi* with a defined and extraordinary technical practice.[4]

It has been the demonstrated ability of *liyuanxi* to use traditional forms to create new scripts that has lifted it above other important traditional southern theatres, in terms of artistic achievement as well as in national and international profile. A century after many modernizing Chinese intellectuals consigned *xiqu* to the rubbish bin of history – where they placed many other important elements of traditional Chinese culture – the concerted efforts of several generations of one ensemble have repeatedly shown that *xiqu* is not only alive but also productive, relevant and ineluctably contemporary.

NOTES

Introduction

1   I here follow Elizabeth Wichmann-Walczak and others in regarding 'opera' as ultimately 'a misleading term for the range of theatrical techniques that distinguish these forms', even if it is unlikely that *xiqu* will soon replace 'Chinese opera' in non-specialist parlance. Elizabeth Wichmann-Walczak, 'Remembering the Past in the Shanghai Jingju Company's King Lear', in *Shakespeare in Hollywood, Asia, and Cyberspace*, ed. Alexander Cheng-Yuan Huang and Charles Stanley Ross (West Lafayette: Purdue University Press, 2009), 183–94. The idea that *xiqu* is best described in English as 'Chinese opera' also leads individual *xiqu* genres to be identified as types of opera, so that 2019 performances in Hong Kong were in English advertised as being by the Experimental Theatre of Liyuan Opera of Fujian.

2   For a recent study of theatre at the Qing court, see Liana Chen, *Staging for the Emperors: A History of Qing Court Theatre, 1683–1923* (Amherst: Cambria Press, 2021).

3   This has given rise to numerous metaphors of *liyuanxi* as a fossil, or a cultural artefact such as the Dunhuang caves. Su Yingmi 蘇英蜜, 'Tan Liyuanxi de jicheng yu gaige 談梨園戲的繼承與改革' [On the Transmission and Reform of Liyuan Theatre], *Fujian yishu* 2 (1999): 12; Lianhe zaobao 聯合早報, 'Dunhuang xianzi xiafan lai – Fujian liyuanxi jin ci yi jia 敦煌仙子下凡來 – 福建梨園戲僅此一家' [Immortals of Dunhuang Come Down to Earth – A Single Fujian Liyuanxi Troupe], *Lianhe zaobao*, 23 October 1991, 50.

4   Robin Ruizendaal, whose field research was conducted in Quanzhou between 1991 and 1995, judged that the term 'fossil' 'may sound cynical in the context of these [FPLET] performances, but it is the most appropriate description'

NOTES

(*Marionette Theatre in Quanzhou* [Boston and Leiden: Brill, 2006], 178) for the period, making the revival both of traditional repertoire and newly written plays in the last quarter-century all the more remarkable.

5   Hugh R. Clark, *Community, Trade, and Networks: Southern Fujian Province from the Third to the Thirteenth Century* (Cambridge: Cambridge University Press, 2002), 168.

6   Christopher Wake, 'The Great Ocean-Going Ships of Southern China in the Age of Chinese Maritime Voyaging to India, Twelfth to Fifteenth Centuries', *International Journal of Maritime History* 9, no. 2 (1997): 51–81.

7   Marco Polo, *The Travels of Marco Polo*, annotated and ed. Henri Cordier, trans. Henry Yule (London: John Murray, 2018), 335.

8   Richard Pearson, Li Min and Li Guo, 'Quanzhou Archaeology: A Brief Review', *International Journal of Historical Archaeology* 6 (2002): 23–59.

9   Roderich Ptak, 'Quanzhou: At the Northern Edge of a Southeast Asian "Mediterranean"?' in *The Emporium of the World: Maritime Quanzhou, 1000–1400*, ed. Angela Schottenhammer (Leiden: Brill, 2001), 395–428.

10   James K. Chin, 'Merchants, Envoys, Brokers and Pirates: Hokkien Connections in Pre-modern Maritime Asia', in *Offshore Asia*, ed. Fujita Kayoko, Momoki Shiro and Anthony Reid (Singapore: ISEAS Publishing, 2013), 65–7.

11   Caroline Chia, *Hokkien Theatre across the Seas* (Singapore: Springer, 2019); Kaori Fushiki and Robin Ruizendaal, eds, *Potehi: Glove Puppet Theatre in Southeast Asia and Taiwan* (Taipei: Taiyuan Publishing, 2016).

12   The provincial capital Fuzhou, too, is bigger than Quanzhou, and Putian is roughly the same size as Quanzhou, but though also in Fujian they are not in the Minnan region and do not speak Hokkien.

13   For instance, Henry Sy of the Philippines, at his death in 2019 the richest man in that country.

14   Unn Målfrid Rolandsen, *Leisure and Power in Urban China: Everyday Life in a Chinese City* (London: Routledge, 2011), 21.

NOTES

15 Picus Sizhi Ding, *Southern Min (Hokkien) as a Migrating Language: A Comparative Study of Language Shift and Maintenance across National Borders* (Berlin: Springer, 2015), 2.

16 Ding, *Southern Min (Hokkien)*, 3. There was even a period in late nineteenth-century Taiwan where there was serious community violence between the Quanzhou and the Zhangzhou arrivals, for which see Stevan Harrell, 'From Xiedou to Yijun, the Decline of Ethnicity in Northern Taiwan, 1885–1895', *Late Imperial China* 11, no. 1 (1990): 99–127.

17 Ruizendaal, *Marionette Theatre in Quanzhou*; Chen Ruitong 陳瑞統, ed., *Quanzhou mu'ou yishu* 泉州木偶藝術 [Quanzhou Puppet Arts] (Xiamen: Lu Jiang chubanshe, 1986); Chia, *Hokkien Theatre across the Seas*, 33–70.

18 Fushiki and Ruizendaal, *Potehi*.

19 Yin-Chen Kang uses a comparison of *Chen San Wuniang* as it appears in a late Qing (1884) script, Cai Youben's recollection in the *Collectanea*, and a 1935 *gezaixi* lyric card as part of an effort to show how Taiwanese theatre began to diverge from its classical Hokkien antecedents; Yin-Chen Kang, 'The Formation of Taiwanese Classical Theatre, 1895–1937' (PhD diss., University of London, 2013), 198–218.

20 Piet van der Loon, *The Classical Theatre and Art Song of South Fukien: A Study of Three Ming Anthologies* (Taipei: SMC Publishing, 1992), 15–16; Caroline Chia, 'Gezai xi in Singapore: Oral Transmission, Improvisation and Dependence on "Fixed Texts"', *CHINOPERL: Journal of Chinese Oral and Performing Literature* 37, no. 1 (2018): 1–41. Its most prominent regional practice is in Manila; Caroline Chia, 'A Preliminary Study of Kaoka 高甲 Playscripts in the Philippines', in *Sinophone Southeast Asia: Sinitic Voices across the Southern Seas*, ed. Tom Hoogervorst and Caroline Chia (Leiden: Brill, 2021), 185–209.

21 Huei-Yuan Belinda Chang, 'A Theatre of Taiwaneseness: Politics, Ideologies, and Gezaixi', *TDR* 41, no. 2 (1997): 111–29; Hsiao-Mei Hsieh, 'Across the Strait: History, Performance and Gezaixi in China and Taiwan' (PhD diss., Northwestern University, 2008).

NOTES 113

22 Although based on a Buddhist sutra, this genre was historically performed mainly as part of Daoist ritual. It is also known as *shigongxi* 師公戲, *shigong* being a term for a Daoist priest.

23 The term *nanyin* predominates in Fujian use; *nanguan* in Taiwan. In earlier records, this practice was also locally called *nanqu* 南曲 (southern melodies). But since *nanqu* has other specific meanings elsewhere in *xiqu*, this usage has been retired. To further complicate matters, there is a Cantonese vocal and orchestral practice also known as *nanyin*, which is not closely related. This practice is sometimes rendered into English according to Cantonese pronunciations such as *lam yin*.

24 Cloris Sau-Ping Lim, 'Nanyin Musical Culture in Southern Fujian, China: Adaptation and Continuity' (PhD diss., University of London, 2014), 102.

25 Rolandsen, *Leisure and Power in Urban China*, 25.

26 Wang Renjie 王仁傑, 'Gu, gu, gu 孤, 古, 固' [Solitary, Ancient, Stubborn], in *Qing xi cangsheng shizhi chuantong* 情系蒼生矢志傳統 [Ties of Love Bind the People to Tradition], ed. Fujian sheng liyuanxi chuancheng zhongxin, Quanzhou shi xiju yanjiusuo and Wang Renjie xiansheng qinshu (Quanzhou: FPLET, 2021), 109–19. This source is a commemorative booklet produced by the troupe, commemorating Wang's life and work on the occasion of the first anniversary of his death.

27 The passage from the *New Book of Tang* reads 'The Emperor knew the laws of melody, and loved dharma songs, and selected three hundred musicians and taught them in the Pear Garden. If anyone was wrong, the emperor would certainly correct them, and the troupe was called "The Emperor's Disciples of the Pear Garden." Several hundred palace maidens also became disciples of the Pear Garden, and lived in the Yichun North Courtyard'; Ouyang Xiu 歐陽修 and Song Qi 宋祁, *Xin Tangshu* 新唐書 [New Book of Tang] (Beijing: Zhonghua shuju, 1975 [1060]), *zhi* 12.12.

28 Tang imperial patronage is also notable, given the later contempt of actors. See Colin Mackerras, 'Peking Opera before the Twentieth Century', *Comparative Drama* 28, no. 1 (1994): 30.

114 NOTES

29 Judith T. Zeitlin, 'Music and Performance in Hong Sheng's *Palace of Lasting Life*', in *Trauma and Transcendence in Early Qing Literature*, ed. Wilt L. Idema, Wai-yee Li and Ellen Widmer (Leiden: Brill, 2006), 462. For this reason, 'Pear Garden' and the alternate translation 'Pear Orchard' have been used in English for other *xiqu* projects and ensembles unrelated to *liyuanxi* that are actually concerned with *jingju* and *kunqu*, notably the Toronto-based Little Pear Garden Collective; Dongshin Chang, 'Performing Traditions and Diasporic Efforts: The Kunqu Society and Little Pear Garden Collective', in *Asian Canadian Theatre*, ed. Nina Lee Aquino and Ric Knowles (Toronto: Playwrights Canada Press, 2011).

30 Ruizendaal, *Marionette Theatre in Quanzhou*, 261.

31 Pan Rongyang 潘榮陽, 'Ming Qing Min-Tai diqu Lei Haiqing xinyang xingsheng tan wei 明清閩台地區雷海青信仰興盛探微' [Brief Exploration of the Rise of the Cult of Lei Haiqing in Ming and Qing Fujian and Taiwan], *Zhongguo Daojiao* 2 (2006): 37–9.

32 Ruizendaal, *Marionette Theatre in Quanzhou*, 261–84; Chia, *Hokkien Theatre across the Seas*, 36.

33 Chu Renhuo 褚人獲, *Sui Tang yanyi* 隋唐演義 [Romance of Sui and Tang Dynasties], Chapter 93, 1695. Available online: https://ctext.org/wiki.pl?if=en&chapter=823084&remap=gb. Translations from Chinese are by the author except where otherwise noted.

34 Lin Qingxi 林慶熙, Zheng Qingshui 鄭清水 and Liu Xiangru 劉湘如, *Fujianxi Shilu* 福建戲史錄 [Historical Records of Theatre in Fujian] (Fuzhou: Fujian renmin chubanshe, 1983), 6–7.

35 For a translation of an account about Lei as a Quanzhou man summoned to play a jade flute sent to Tang Minghuang by Heaven, see Poh Sim Plowright, *Mediums, Puppets, and the Human Actor in the Theatres of the East* (Lewiston: Edwin Mellen Press, 2002), 51–3.

36 Ruizendaal, *Marionette Theatre in Quanzhou*, 261.

37 Van der Loon, *The Classical Theatre and Art Song of South Fukien*, 19.

38 This is to some degree in contrast to the usual thinking around *xiqu* casting, in which technical aptitude and stage look were

NOTES 115

long determining, rather than actor age. In other genres, too, however recent decades have seen a valorization of youth over experience.

39 Thus, one of the difficulties in *liyuanxi* research is the fact that the genre name means 'theatre of the Pear Garden' and *xiqu* performers in general are known as 'disciples of the Pear Garden' (*liyuan zidi* 梨園子弟). It is only in the Hokkien cultural sphere that reference to 'Pear Garden' will be taken to mean this particular genre rather than the stage in general. The choice of the name of the genre has not been universally welcomed, with notably Piet van der Loon on several occasions registering his disapproval in print.

Chapter 1

1 A useful sourcebook for the history of theatre in the region is Lin, Zheng and Liu, *Fujian xi shilu*, but it is often not clear how or even whether modern categories of genre can be sensibly applied. The fact that the theatre is often called a 'remnant', a 'fossil' or a 'lingering echo' of *nanxi* is intended as an acknowledgement of the genre's historic importance and authenticity, although it may simultaneously do a disservice to the genre's contemporary vitality. The same vocabulary is deployed for the equally venerable (but today less prominent) genre of *puxianxi* to the immediate north in Putian and Xianyou. For *kunqu* scholars' efforts to 'triumphantly extend[s]' the history of the musical genre, see Xu Peng, 'The Music Teacher: The Professionalization of Singing and the Development of Erotic Vocal Style during Late Ming China', *Harvard Journal of Asiatic Studies* 75, no. 2 (2015): 259–97.

2 Wang Renjie quotes the pre-eminent Western scholar in this area, the late Piet van der Loon, as joking that 'soon it'll be traced back to pre-history'. Wang Renjie 王仁傑, 'Xu 序' [Introduction], in *Liyuanxi shihua* 梨園戲史話 (Historical Accounts of Liyuanxi), ed. Ye Xiaomei (Beijing: Shehui kexue wenxian chubanshe, 2015), 4. Wang, always wily, might have found it amusing to put this barb in a safe and respectable (and

116 NOTES

deceased) foreigner's mouth. Since Wang too is now dead we are left just with the *bon mot*. That said, Wang is elsewhere in his writing more willing than van der Loon to credit Ming records as representing evidence of *liyuanxi* performance.

3   Piet van der Loon, *The Classical Theatre and Art Song of South Fukien: A Study of Three Ming Anthologies* (Taipei: SMC Publishing, 1992).

4   Colin Mackerras, *Chinese Drama: A Historical Survey* (Beijing: New World Press, 1990). At much the same time, the four-act 'miscellany drama' (*zaju* 雜劇) scripts of the north also developed. *Zaju* played no direct role in the development of what became *liyuanxi*, but are the best-known category of early Chinese drama, not least because their brevity made them easier to translate, anthologize and teach. For an introduction to *zaju*, consult Stephen H. West and Wilt L. Idema, eds, *The Orphan of Zhao and Other Yuan Plays: The Earliest Known Versions* (New York: Columbia University Press, 2014).

5   Mei Sun, 'The Division between "Nanxi" and "Chuanqi"', *American Journal of Chinese Studies* 5, no. 2 (1998): 248–56.

6   Van der Loon, *The Classical Theatre and Art Song of South Fukien*, 7. Because so few Hokkien texts of such early date remain, they have also proven of enduring interest to linguists. See Henning Klöter, *Written Taiwanese* (Wiesbaden: Otto Harrassowitz Verlag, 2005), 58–64.

7   Liu Nianzi 劉念玆, *Nanxi xin zheng* 南戲新證 [New Evidential Interpretation of Southern Drama] (Beijing: Zhonghua shuju, 1986).

8   Mei Sun, 'Exploring the Historical Development of Nanxi, Southern Theater', *CHINOPERL: Journal of Chinese Oral and Performing Literature* 24, no. 1 (2002): 40–1.

9   The four as usually listed are *The Lute* (*Pipa ji* 琵琶記), *The Thorn Hairpin* (*Jingchai ji* 荊釵記), *The White Hare* (*Baitu ji* 白兔記) and *Killing a Dog* (*Shagou ji* 殺狗記). In *liyuanxi*, where traditional repertoire typically bears the name of the male protagonists, these narratives are respectively *Cai Bojie* 蔡伯喈, *Wang Shipeng* 王十朋, *Liu Zhiyuan* 劉智遠 and *Sun Rong* 孫榮. Scenes from all are still in repertoire, and a

one-night version of *Cai Bojie* based on the *Collectanea* records was revived in 2015 and is still in repertoire.

10 Yu Weimin 俞為民, 'Song Yuan "Si da nanxi" zai liyuanxi zhong de liuchuan yu bianyi 宋元 "四大南戲" 在梨園戲中的流傳與變異' [The Alterations in the Liyuan Opera Adaptations of 'The Four Great Nanxi Plays'], *Wenhua yishu yanjiu* 12, no. 1 (2019): 64–76.

11 Yu, 'Song Yuan', 76.

12 Van der Loon, *The Classical Theatre and Art Song of South Fukien*. Like Chinese scholars, van der Loon concludes that 'of all the existing regional genres' what he calls the 'classical theatre of South Fukien … remained the most faithful to early Southern Drama flourishing from the thirteenth to the sixteenth century' (i); Cai Tiemin 蔡鐵民, 'Ming chuanqi "Lizhi ji" yanbian chutan – Jian tan nanxi zai Fujian de yixiang 明傳奇《荔支記》演變初探 —— 兼談南戲在福建的遺響' [Preliminary Thoughts on the Development of the Ming Chuanqi Script The Tale of the Lychee – Also on the Echoes of Nanxi in Fujian], *Xiamen daxue xuebao* (zhexue shehui kexue ban) 3 (1979): 41.

13 Zhongguo xiqu yanjiuyuan 中國戲曲研究院, ed., *Zhongguo gudian xiqu lunzhu jicheng di san ji* 中國古典戲曲論著集成第三集 [Classical Chinese Xiqu Treatises, vol. 3] (Beijing: Zhongguo xiju chubanshe, 1959), 235–57; Liusha 流沙, *Mingdai nanxi shengqiang yuanliu kao bian* 明代南戲聲腔源流考辨 [Research on the Sources of Ming Dynasty Southern Drama's Vocal Music] (Taipei: Caituan faren Shi Hezheng minsu wenhua jijinhui, 1999), 466–70. For the transcripts of actors in the 1950s, see the *Quanzhou Traditional Xiqu Collectanea* 泉州傳統戲曲叢刊 ed. Quanzhou difang xiqu yanjiu she 泉州地方戲曲研究社, of which more below.

14 Qian Nanyang 錢南揚, ed., *Song Yuan xiwen jiyi* 宋元戲文輯佚 [Collected Song and Yuan Dynasty Nanxi Fragments] (Shanghai: Shanghai gudian wenxue chubanshe, 1956).

15 Ying-fen Wang, 'Tune Identity and Compositional Process in Zhongbei Songs: A Semiotic Analysis of *Nanguan* Vocal Music' (PhD diss., University of Pittsburgh, 1992), 7.

NOTES

16 The full title is *Reprint of the Complete Tale of the Lychees and the Mirror for Five Role Types, Containing Chaozhou and Quanzhou Elements, Inserted Humorous Verses, Enriched with Northern Tunes and a Brothel Scene* [*Chongkan wuse Chao-Quan chake zengru shici Beiqu goulan Lijing ji xiwen quanji* 重刊五色潮泉插科增入詩詞北曲勾欄荔鏡記戲文全集]. The fact that it is a reprint suggests that the narrative was circulating for some time before, and already enjoyed a high degree of local popularity.

17 Kurata Junnosuke 倉田淳之助 sent Wu the Tenri copies, while the Oxford copies reached him through Jao Tsung-I 饒宗頤. The PRC became aware of the manuscripts via a Japanese tour of actor-intellectuals Mei Lanfang 梅蘭芳 and Ouyang Yuqian 歐陽予倩 in 1956. In point of fact, the scholar Hsiang Ta (Xiang Da 向達) had included notes on the Oxford text in his 1936 account of the Bodleian's Chinese collections, but it does not seem that anyone took notice of this account before Wu's publications. Since Hsiang himself was not familiar with contemporary Fujian theatre, he did not connect it to the living stage. Hsiang Ta 向達, '*Yingya suozhi – ji Niujin suo cang de wenshu* 瀛涯瑣志–記牛津所藏的中文書' [Trivial Records from the Ocean's Shores – On the Chinese Books Held in Oxford], *Guoli Peiping tushuguan guankan* X/5 (1936), 9–44. See pp. 27–9 for the *liyuanxi* materials. In 2021, the Bodleian copy was digitized, and is available as Sinica 34/1 and 34/2.

18 In the same year, Piet van der Loon discovered a 1581 Chaozhou version of the text in Vienna, now digitally available through the Austrian National Library https://digital.onb.ac.at/OnbViewer/viewer.faces?doc=ABO_%2BZ43240502.

19 Zheng Guoquan 鄭國權, '"Li jing ji" san bian 《荔鏡記》三辨' [Three Arguments about the *Story of the Lychees and the Mirror*], in *Xishi bian* 戲史辨 [Theatre History Debates], vol. 4, ed. Hu Ji and Luo Di (Beijing: Zhongguo xiju chubanshe, 2004), 298–301.

20 The three van der Loon texts were published in facsimile with a scholarly introduction in 1992 in his work *The Classical Theatre and Art Song of South Fukien* (also available in a Chinese-language edition, with the introduction translated into Chinese).

NOTES 119

21 Yibo Wang, 'Liyuan Opera *Lizhiji*: New Materials, Stories and Insights' (PhD diss., University of Edinburgh, 2019), 36–41.

22 Van der Loon, *The Classical Theatre and Art Song of South Fukien*, 3–14.

23 Chinfa Lien, 'Interface of Modality and the tit[4] 得 Constructions in Southern Min: A Case Study of their Developments from Earlier Southern Min in the Ming and Qing to Modern Taiwanese Southern Min', *Language and Linguistics* 12, no. 4 (2011): 745. See Chinfa Lien and Alain Peyraube, eds, *Diachronic Perspectives and Synchronic Variation in Southern Min* (New York: Routledge, 2020) for several recent uses.

24 Andrea S. Goldman, 'The Nun Who Wouldn't Be: Representations of Female Desire in Two Performance Genres of "Si Fan"', *Late Imperial China* 22, no. 1 (2001): 71–138.

25 Kaori Fushiki, 'Nanyin and the Singaporean Culture: The Creation of Intangible Cultural Heritage in Singapore and Intergenerational Contrasts', in *Transglobal Sounds: Music, Youth and Migration*, ed. João Sardinha and Ricardo Campos (London: Bloomsbury, 2016), 93–112.

26 Quanzhou difang xiqu yanjiu she 泉州地方戲曲研究社, *Quanzhou chuantong xiqu congshu* 泉州傳統戲曲叢書 [Quanzhou Traditional Xiqu Collectanea] (Beijing: Zhongguo xiju chubanshe, 2000). The remaining six volumes are devoted to puppet theatres.

27 Nationally, the writing 劉知遠 is more common, but this orthography seems more common in Quanzhou.

28 Chia, *Hokkien Theatre across the Seas*, 18.

29 Van der Loon, *The Classical Theatre and Art Song of South Fukien*, 22.

30 Lin, Zheng and Liu, *Fujian xi shilu*, 42–3. It is likely that the Spanish embassy sent from Manila in 1579 saw both. See van der Loon, *The Classical Theatre and Art Song of South Fukien*, 21–2.

31 Lin, Zheng and Liu, *Fujian xi shilu*, 47.

32 Translation from van der Loon, *The Classical Theatre and Art Song of South Fukien*, 21. The Chinese source, *Miscellaneous Notes from Quannan* (Quannan zazhi 泉南雜志), is available

120 NOTES

in the *Siku quanshu*, in Wikisource, and numerous other print and electronic versions.

33 Zhu Jingying 朱景英, *Haidong zhaji* 海東札記 [Notebooks of Haidong] 3 (Chinese Text Project, 1773); Lin, Zheng and Liu, *Fujian xi shilu*, 109.

34 Ya-xian Xu, *Sounds from the Other Side: The Operatic Interaction between Colonial Taiwan and China during the Early Twentieth Century*, trans. Jo-hsuan Wang (Taipei: SMC Publishing, 2013), 16. For a translation of Yu's poem, see van der Loon, *The Classical Theatre and Art Song of South Fukien*, 28.

35 Troupes are reported as visiting in 1899 and 1902, presumably from Quanzhou. Xu, *Sounds from the Other Side*, 88–9.

36 Lian Heng 連橫, *Taiwan tongshi* 台湾通史 [A General History of Taiwan], ed. Lian Yatang (Taipei: Taiwan yinhang jingji yanjiusuo, 1985).

37 Lin, Zheng and Liu, *Fujian xi shilu*, 155–6. For an example of banning of the same narrative by child actors in Penghu in 1879, see Chia, *Hokkien Theatre across the Seas*, 42.

38 Ye Xiaomei 葉曉梅, *Liyuanxi shihua* 梨園戲史話 [Notes on Liyuanxi History] (Beijing: Shehui kexue wenxian chubanshe, 2015), 15.

39 Van der Loon, *The Classical Theatre and Art Song of South Fukien*, 24.

40 Chia, *Hokkien Theatre across the Seas*, 156.

41 Xu, *Sounds from the Other Side*, 238–9.

42 For extensive records of late Qing and Republican troupe names and dates, see Zhuang Changjiang 莊長江, *Quanzhou xi ban* 泉州戲班 [Theatre Troupes of Quanzhou] (Fuzhou: Fujian renmin chubanshe, 2006), 3–18.

43 Wu Jieqiu 吳捷秋, *Liyuanxi yishu shilun* 梨園戲藝術史論 [A History of Liyuanxi Artistry] (Beijing: Zhongguo xiju chubanshe, 1996), 345–96.

44 Mei Sun, 'Performances of *nanxi*', *Asian Theatre Journal* 13, no. 2 (1996): 153–7.

45 Chia-Lan Chang, 'Family Matters: Women's Negotiation with Confucian Family Ethics in Qing and Republican China'

NOTES

(PhD diss., University of Southern California, 2007). One sign of this might be the Qing prominence of Quanzhou as an important site for the chaste widow cult. Cai, 'Ming chuanqi "Lizhi ji" yanbian chutan', 33. This may go some distance to explaining why Wang Renjie's most famous works revolved so substantially around the question of widow chastity.

46 Cai, 'Ming chuanqi "Lizhi ji" yanbian chutan', 33.

47 1984 interview with Lin Luanzhen 林鸞珍 (b. 1911), Yan Zihe 顏梓和, compiler, 'Gezaixi ban "Shuang zhu feng" de caifang ziliao 歌仔戲班"雙珠鳳"的採訪資料' [Interview Materials of the 'Double-Pearl Double-Phoenix Troupe'], in *Gezaixi ziliao huibian* 歌仔戲資料匯編 [Gezaixi Resource Compendium], ed. Chen Geng, Zeng Xuewen and Wu Anhui (Beijing: Guangming ribao chubanshe, 1997), 126–7.

48 The most comprehensive account and cataloguing of Fujian theatre abroad, including non-Hokkien genres, is Wang Hanmin's 2011 work, *Fujian xiqu haiwai chuanbo yanjiu* 福建戲曲海外傳播研究 [Research on Fujian Xiqu's Performance Abroad] (Beijing: Zhongguo shehui kexue chubanshe).

49 With the agreement of the troupe and the actors, I conducted several interviews in June 2013 in Quanzhou on the understanding that the quotes would not be given named attributions. The quote here is among them. Other ones are simply given as 'Quanzhou, FPLET, June 2013'.

50 Nancy Guy, *Peking Opera and Politics in Taiwan* (Champaign: University of Illinois Press, 2005).

51 Kim Hunter Gordon, 'Contesting Traditional *Luzi* ("Choreographic Paths"): A Performance-Based Study of Kunqu' (PhD diss., University of London, 2016), 143.

52 Xiaomei Chen, Tarryn Li-Min Chun and Siyuan Liu, *Rethinking Chinese Socialist Theaters of Reform: Performance Practice and Debate in the Mao Era* (Ann Arbor: University of Michigan Press, 2021).

53 Wang Wei 王偉, 'Fujian xiqu gaige yu gujin lijing qingyuan 福建戲曲改革與古今荔鏡情緣' [Fujianese Opera Reform and Versions of The Lychees and the Mirror through the Ages], *Yiyuan* 6 (2016): 17; Jeremy E. Taylor, 'Lychees and Mirrors: Local

Opera, Cinema, and Diaspora in the Chinese Cultural Cold War', *Twentieth-Century China* 43, no. 2 (2018): 169.

54   Genre names are seldom critically examined but can have complex histories and important implications, especially if the genre exists or existed both inside and outside the PRC, as has been richly documented for the case of the genre now in Chinese universally called *jingju* (Peking Opera), but which underwent various name changes in Taiwan as cross-Strait dynamics shifted. Nancy A. Guy, 'Peking Opera as "National Opera" in Taiwan: What's in a Name?', *Asian Theatre Journal* 12, no. 1 (1995): 85–103. Though the stakes are lower, the same is true of *liyuanxi*, as will become clearer when its Taiwanese relatives or branches are discussed.

55   Wu, *Liyuanxi yishu shilun*, 397–401.

56   Thus, while a critical attitude towards the mediation and construction of tradition is welcome and necessary, it is not quite correct to claim that 'All we have now of the Liyuan libretti are mostly transcripts made in the 1990s by Wu Jieqiu working with veteran performers familiar with the tradition' (Chia, *Hokkien Theatre across the Seas*, 19). Besides the texts discovered by Piet van der Loon, which can probably be considered scripts for *liyuanxi* as long as one keeps in mind the history of the generic terms, the bulk of *liyuanxi* libretti as written can be traced to oral accounts of traditional repertoire made by actors such as Cai Youben and He Shumin in the 1950s.

57   Wu, *Liyuanxi yishu shilun*, 413–18; Huang Wenjuan 黄文娟, 'Xigai shiqi de "Chen San Wuniang" 戲改時期的《陳三五娘》' [*Chen San and Wuniang* during Opera Reform], *Fujian yishu* 福建藝術 5 (2015): 32–6; Taylor, 'Lychees and Mirrors', 169.

58   Wu's *Liyuanxi yishu shilun*, which was published in two Mainland editions as well as in Taiwan, remains the central monograph for the academic study of *liyuanxi*. His institutional embeddedness – and direct participation in the troupe's establishment and in 1950s repertoire – is both a great strength and a significant limitation of his work.

59   Wilt L. Idema, 'The Emergence of Regional Opera on the National Stage', in *A New Literary History of Modern China*,

NOTES 123

ed. David Der-wei Wang (Cambridge: Harvard University Press, 2018), 585–90. An excellent study of another genre and narrative that in this way reached national attention is Wilt Idema's *The Metamorphosis of Tianxian pei: Local Opera under the Revolution (1949–1956)* (Hong Kong: The Chinese University of Hong Kong Press, 2015). As with *liyuanxi*, one of the results was cinematic adaptation.

60 Wu, *Liyuanxi yishu shilun*, 25.

61 Zhang Aiding 張艾丁, 'Liyuanxi "Chen San Wuniang" 梨園戲"陳三五娘"' [The *Liyuanxi* Version of *Chen San and Wuniang*], *Xiju bao* 9 (1955): 16.

62 Zhang, 'Liyuanxi'.

63 Su Yanshi 蘇彥石, 'Qiangjiu jicheng chuangxin – Fujian sheng Liyuanxi shiyan jutuan wushi nian huigu 搶救·繼承·創新——福建省梨園戲實驗劇團五十年回顧' [Rescue, Transmit, Innovate – Looking Back on Fifty Years of the FPLET], *Fujian yishu* (2003): 44–6.

64 Dai Bufan 戴不凡, 'Di er ge Su Wu – Liyuanxi "Zhu bian lengshan ji" guan hou 第二個蘇武——梨園戲《朱弁冷山記》觀後' [A Second Su Wu – The Liyuan Play *Zhu Bian on the Cold Mountain*], *Xiju bao* (1959): 22. That reception was renewed upon its revival in 2010 as Zhu Bian, with Wang Renjie reworking Lin Rensheng's adaptation. Xie Zichou 謝子丑, 'Shusheng shi shou Han jia jie – Liyuanxi 'Zhu Bian' Zhong de aiguo qijie 書生誓守漢家節——梨園戲《朱弁》中的愛國氣節' [A Scholar Keeping Han Integrity – Patriotic Integrity in Liyuanxi's *Zhu Bian*], *Fujian yishu* 1 (2010): 67–8.

65 Siyuan Liu, 'Theatre Reform as Censorship: Censoring Traditional Theatre in China in the Early 1950s', *Theatre Journal* 61, no. 3 (2009): 387–406; Anne Elizabeth Rebull, 'Theaters of Reform and Remediation: Xiqu (Chinese Opera) in the Mid-twentieth Century' (PhD diss., University of Chicago, 2017).

66 Zheng Guoquan 鄭國權, 'Huoxia qu, chuanxialai 活下去, 傳下來' [Live On, Pass On], in *Nanxi yixiang* 南戲遺響 [Lingering Notes of Southern Drama], ed. Quanzhou difang xiqu yanjiu she (Beijing: Zhongguo xiju chubanshe, 1991), 253.

124 NOTES

67 Su, 'Tan Liyuanxi', 13. *Wandering through Green Mountains* was likely adapted from other *xiqu* scripts.

68 Of the three pre-Cultural Revolution troupes, only the Quanzhou and the Nan'an troupes were reestablished, and these were eventually merged in Quanzhou to create the present-day FPLET.

69 Su, 'Qiangjiu'. The final name has stuck, even though the troupe is since 2012 technically a 'transmission centre', perhaps a response to the push in the early 2010s for the 'marketization' of *xiqu*, a policy since largely reversed.

70 Members of the troupe recall this being a popular show in the early post-Mao era, with months of performance in 1977 and 1978. In addition, it may have been symbolic for *xiqu* circles at the time, since *Fifteen Strings of Cash* was associated with the rescue of *kunqu* and its inclusion into the social apparatus after the destructive Civil War. It is furthermore worth noting the borrowing from a distant genre, a common feature in all *xiqu* genres, yet one often elided in a discourse which tends to privilege genre independence. For the role of this play in PRC *xiqu* reform, see Rebull, 'Theaters of Reform and Remediation'.

71 Su also used the name Su Yanshuo 蘇彥碩; the divergent characters are homophonous in the Quanzhou dialect.

72 Su Yanshi 蘇彥石, 'Fujian sheng de zuijia nü yanyuan Zeng Jingping 福建省的最佳女演員曾靜萍' [Zeng Jingping, the Best Actress of Fujian Province], *Xiju bao 5* (1988): 60.

73 Su, 'Fujian sheng de zuijia nü yanyuan Zeng Jingping', 60.

74 Wang, *Fujian xiqu haiwai chuanbo yanjiu*, 36; Fujian sheng difangzhi bianzuan weiyuanhui 福建省地方志編纂委員會, 'Duiwai wenhua jiaoliu 對外文化交流' [International Cultural Exchange], in *Fujian sheng zhi: Wenhua yishu zhi* 福建省志：文化藝術志 [Culture and Arts Gazetteer for Fujian Province], ed. Fujian sheng difangzhi bianzuan weiyuanhui (Fuzhou: Fujian renmin chubanshe, 2008), 618.

75 Huang Chaosong 黃朝松, 'Liang'an liyuanxi chuanxi jihua zhi xiankuang yu weilai zhanwang 兩岸梨園戲傳習計畫之現況與未來展望' [Present Situation and Future Developments of the Transmission Program for 'Liyuan' Opera on Both Sides of the

Strait], in *Chuantong yishu yantao hui: Lunwen ji* 傳統藝術研討會：論文集 [Traditional Arts Conference: Collected Essays], ed. Guoli chuantong yishu zhongxin choubei chu (Yilan: Guoli chuantong yishu zhongxin choubei chu, 1998), 61; Wang, *Fujian xiqu haiwai chuanbo yanjiu*, 36.

76 Wang Renjie 王仁傑, 'Liyuan shide jiushidiao fanzuo xinshengchang duanchang – xiju xinde zatan 梨園拾得舊時調翻作新聲唱斷腸 – 習劇心得雜談' [Collecting Old Melodies in a Pear Garden, Turning them into Heart-rending New Voices: Random Discoveries from a Life in Theatre], *Juben* 12 (1997): 3.

77 Wang, 'Liyuan shide jiushidiao fanzuo xinshengchang duanchang', 4.

78 Wang Renjie 王仁傑 and Tan Huafu 譚華孚, 'Xiqu wenhua de fanben yu kaixin: Yin Chen Zhongzi er qi de duihua 戲曲文化的返本與開新：因《陳仲子》而起的對話' [Return to Roots and New Shoots in Xiqu Culture: A Dialogue beginning from Chen Zhongzi], *Fujian xiju* (1991): 34.

79 Lü Xiaoping 呂效平, 'Dong Sheng yu Li Shi: Wang Renjie he ta de Dong Sheng yu Li Shi《董生與李氏》：王仁傑和他的《董生與李氏》' [Scholar Dong and Madam Li: Wang Renjie and His Scholar Dong and Madam Li], in *Fanbenkaixin: Wang Renjie juzuo yanjiu lunwenxuan* 返本開新：王仁傑劇作研究論文選 [Returning to the Roots, Putting out New Shoots: A Collection of Essays on Wang Renjie's Dramatic Works], ed. Xue Ruolin, Liu Zhen and Fan Biyun (Beijing: Wenhua yishu chubanshe, 2012), 292–9.

80 She typically uses this platform as a way to highlight the importance of traditional culture and the arts. Huang Qiongfen 黃瓊芬, 'Zeng Jingping: Rang xin linian hua wei fei yichuan cheng xin liliang 曾靜萍：讓新理念化為非遺傳承新力量' [Zeng Jingping: Let New Conceptualizing Become the New Strength of Intangible Culture Transmission], *Dongnan wang*, 14 March 2021.

81 Zeng Jingping 曾静萍, 'Ba liyuanxi de jingsui hua ru xieye 把梨園戲的精髓化入血液' [Letting the Essence of Liyuanxi Flow into the Bloodstream], *Zhongguo xiqu xueyuan xuebao* 37, no. 4 (2016): 1. One younger artist, recruited from the countryside at the age of twelve, told me that due to the 'pear garden'

126 NOTES

name, she assumed she was going to be trained for work in an orchard.

82 Zeng, 'Ba liyuanxi de jingsui hua ru xieye', 1.

83 Lin Ruiwu 林瑞武, 'Shi xi Zeng Jingping de biaoyan yishu 試析曾靜萍的表演藝術' [An Analysis of Zeng Jingping's Art as a Performer], *Fujian xiju 5* (1998): 9.

84 The locality of one's household registration (*hukou* 戶口) constitutes an important determinant of social status and access to services in the PRC.

85 Lim, 'Nanyin Musical Culture in Southern Fujian', 237. The training institution was re-established in 1978 as a branch of the province's Fujian yishu xuexiao 福建藝術學校 [Fujian Arts School]. In 1998, the school moved to its present premises; a year later, it became a branch of Fujian Province Arts School and renamed Fujian yishu xuexiao Quanzhou fenxiao 福建藝術學校泉州分校 [Fujian Arts School, Quanzhou Branch], but in 2004 was turned into an independent school within the public education system known as Fujiansheng Quanzhou yishu xuexiao 福建省泉州藝術學校 [Fujian Province Quanzhou Arts School], and usually simply referred to as 'Yixiao', art school.

86 Quanzhou, FPLET, June 2013.

87 Huifen Shen, 'Engendering Chinese Migration History: "Left-Behind Wives of the Nanyang Migrants" in Quanzhou before and after the Pacific War' (PhD diss., National University of Singapore, 2006). By the mid-1970s, both Hong Kong entry requirements and Chinese exit permits for those with relatives abroad had relaxed (Shen, 195–6). Although Quanzhou communities had existed in Hong Kong earlier, most of this migration occurred in the early 1980s. Southeast Asian cities have had large Quanzhou communities since the nineteenth century, and chain migration could resume, though it did so on a much smaller scale than before the Revolution. Leong, 'Bearers of Great Riches'.

88 Fabienne Darge, 'L'art du liyuan ne craint pas la modernité' [Liyuan's Art Is Not Afraid of the Modern], *Le Monde*,

NOTES

127

5 June 2014. Available online: https://www.lemonde.fr/culture/article/2014/06/05/l-art-du-liyuan-ne-craint-pas-la-modernite_4432320_3246.html.

89 Much of the information in this section is derived from group interviews in Quanzhou, FPLET, June 2013.

90 Attempts to teach adults have not been successful, in that graduates from such programmes have not become professional actors.

91 This paragraph is derived from group interviews in Quanzhou, FPLET, June 2013.

92 Lianhe zaobao, 'Dunhuang xianzi xiafan lai – Fujian liyuanxi jin ci yi jia', 50.

93 Patrick Sommier, 'L'Art des nations: Travailler dans un théâtre en Chine et en Russie' [L'Art des Nations: Working in a Theatre in China and in Russia], *KROUM* (18–28 January 2018): 9.

94 Women who have occupied important positions in the *xiqu* establishment include the actors Pei Yanling 裴艷玲 (b. 1947), Bai Shuxian 白淑賢 (b. 1947) and Mao Weitao 茅威濤 (b. 1962), all three of whom play male roles. Thus, even where women have reached high positions within the *xiqu* hierarchy, it is often connected to the performance of masculinity.

95 *Xiqu* audiences are indeed habituated to genres, such as *gezaixi* and Zhejiang *yueju*, in which most often all characters are performed by women. But even in genres where nowadays performers' gender aligns with the roles they play, such as *kunqu*, the exception tends to be for the genteel scholar, as in the case of the two great *kunqu nü xiaosheng* of the post-Mao years, Shi Xiaomei 石小梅 (b. 1949) of Jiangsu and Yue Meiti 岳美緹 (b. 1941) of Shanghai.

96 Chia, *Hokkien Theatre across the Seas*; Beiyu Zhang, *Chinese Theatre Troupes in Southeast Asia: Touring Diaspora, 1900s–1970s* (London: Routledge, 2021); Beiyu Zhang, 'Travelling with Chinese Theatre-Troupes: A "Performative Turn" in Sino-Southeast Asian Interactions', *Asian Theatre Journal* 38, no. 1 (2021): 191–217.

97 Wang, *Fujian xiqu haiwai chuanbo yanjiu*, 205–6.

128 NOTES

98 Bilingual Theatre Programme, 'Fujian Liyuan Opera Troupe – People's Republic of China – Philippine Performance Tour 1986/ Zhongguo Fujian Liyuanxi Shiyan Jutuan – Fangfei yanchu tekan 中國福建梨園戲實驗劇團 – 訪菲演出特刊' [China's Fujian Province Liyuanxi Experimental Theatre – Philippines Tour Special Issue], 1. Held by the Fujian Province Liyuanxi Experimental Theatre Archives.

99 Bilingual Theatre Programme, 'Fujian Liyuan Opera Troupe', 2.

100 FPLET Archives, Philippine Tour Clippings Book; *Shijie Ribao* 世界日報, 16 November 1986. Clippings do not indicate page number.

101 FPLET Archives, A2-004-161-6-39; A2-004-161-2-30.

102 FPLET Archives, Philippine Tour Clippings Book; *Renmin Ribao*, 14 October 1986.

103 Wang, *Fujian xiqu haiwai chuanbo yanjiu*, 323–4.

104 Fujian sheng difangzhi bianzuan weiyuanhui, 'Duiwai wenhua jiaoliu', 615.

105 Fujian sheng difangzhi bianzuan weiyuanhui, 'Duiwai wenhua jiaoliu', 618.

106 Ministry of Culture (Republic of China, Taiwan), 'Nanguanxi yiren 南管戲藝人' [Artists of the Nanguan Stage]. Available online: https://learning.moc.gov.tw/course/2266cd64-0b4a-4f7d-93f8-b27f99d08add/content/ar/02-1/data/downloads/02-1.pdf.

107 Hong Weizhu 洪惟助, '1963 nian Taiwan qizixi peixunban shimo jiyi yingxiang 1963 年台灣七子戲培訓班始末及其影響' [All about the 1963 Taiwanese Child Actor Training Cohort and Its Influence], in *Haixia liang'an liyuanxi xueshu yantaohui lunwenji* 海峽兩岸梨園戲學術研討會論文集 [Cross-strait Liyuanxi Research Conference Essay Collection], ed. Tseng Yong-yih (Taipei: Guoli Zhongzheng wenhu zhongxin, 1998), 3–17.

108 Shi Ruilou 施瑞樓, 'Huainian zhongyao minzu yishu yishi Li Xiangshi xiansheng – Ji Li shi ersan shi 懷念重要民族藝術藝師 李祥石先生 – 記李師二三事' [In Memory of the Important Ethnic Artist, Mister Li Xiangshi – Remembering Two or Three Things about Mister Li], in *Li Xiangshi yishi nanguanxi juben – koushu chuanlu* 李祥石藝師南管戲劇本 – 口述傳錄 [The Li Xiangshi Nanguan Theatre Script – Oral Records], ed.

Shi Ruilou (Taipei: National Taiwan Arts Education Center, 2004), 7–28; Hong Jingyi 洪靜儀, 'Wu Suxia qi jiao xi wutai yanchu ben yanjiu 吳素霞七腳戲舞台演出本研究 [Research on Wu Su-hsia's Qijiaoxi Stage Art]' (PhD diss., National Taipei University, 2011).

109 Cultural Heritage Department of Taichung City, 'Zhongyao chuantong biaoyan yishu – nanguan xiqu – baocun zhe Lin Wu Suxia 重要傳統表演藝術-南管戲曲-保存者林吳素霞' [An Important Traditional Art – Nanguan xiqu – Culture-bearer Lin Wu Su-hsia], *Cultural Heritage Department of Taichung City*, 8 January 2020. Available online: https://www.tchac. taichung.gov.tw/historybuilding?uid=38&pid=126.

110 Ying-fen Wang, 'Lessons from the Past: Nanguan/Nanyin and the Preservation of Intangible Cultural Heritage in Taiwan', in *Music as Intangible Cultural Heritage: Policy, Ideology, and Practice in the Preservation of East Asian Traditions*, ed. Keith Howard (Farnham: Ashgate, 2012), 176.

111 Josh Stenberg, 'Performance Review: Nanguan Meets Modern Chinese Poetry: Wang Xinxin's Nanguan shiyi (Nanguan/Poetic meaning) Taiwan Tour, May 2015', *CHINOPERL: Journal of Chinese Oral and Performing Literature* 34, no. 2 (2015): 179–81; Liao Yuning 廖于瀞, 'Jiangzhicui juchang "Zhu Wen zou gui" yanyi zhi yanjiu 江之翠劇場《朱文走鬼》演藝之研究' [Research on Gang-a-tsui's Performance of Zhu Wen Flees the Ghost] (PhD diss., National Taiwan Normal University, 2011); Shih Cheng-xing 施政昕, 'Lun Han Tang Yuefu de "Luoshen fu" bian yan celüe: Yi changci anpai, yuandian yingyong yu yinyue sheji wei zhongxin 論漢唐樂府的《洛神賦》編演策略:以場次安排、原典應用與音樂設計為中心' [Arrangement and Performance Strategies of 'The Lyric for Lo River Goddess' by Han-Tang Yuefu Music Ensemble: Session Organization, Literary Allusion and Music Design], *Zhongguo wenxue yanjiu* 49 (2020): 41–74.

112 Qian Chenxiang 錢陳翔, 'Cong "Taiwan Han Tang Yuefu" kan nanyin guyue de xin fazhan 從"台灣漢唐樂府"看南音古樂的新發展' [Seeing the New Development of Ancient Southern Music from Taiwan Han-tang Yuefu], *Yinyue tansuo* 4 (2011): 31–4.

113 Liao, 'Jiangzicui juchang "Zhu Wen zou gui" yanyi zhi yanjiu'.

130 NOTES

114 Shzr Ee Tan, 'Unequal Cosmopolitanisms: Staging Singaporean Nanyin in and beyond Asia', in *Asian City Crossings: Pathways of Performance through Hong Kong and Singapore*, ed. Rossella Ferrari and Ashley Thorpe (London: Routledge, 2021), 195–6.

115 Tan, 'Unequal Cosmopolitanisms', 199.

116 Tan, 'Unequal Cosmopolitanisms', 199.

117 The performance seems to have been in conjunction with the special award given to Lü Tongliu 呂同六 (1938–2005), the PRC's principal scholar and translator of Italian literature. One might surmise that the organizers, wishing to include a Chinese theme, reached the FPLET via diplomatic channels; Wang, *Fujian xiqu haiwai chuanbo yanjiu*.

118 David Johnson, 'Report on the International Conference on Chinese Southern Opera (Nanxi) and Mulian Opera: Fukien, 2/26/91–3/5/91', *CHINOPERL: Journal of Chinese Oral and Performing Literature* 16, no. 1 (1992): 207–14.

119 Marcus Tan, 'Fabulous Review: The Global Soul: The Buddha Project by Theatreworks', *The Flying Inkpot*, 21 June 2003. Available online: http://www.inkpotreviews.com/oldInkpot/03revi ews/03revglobsoulbuddproj.html. Since Ong was born to migrants from nearby Putian, one can infer that there is a diasporic angle to his interest in the genres of his ancestral region; Ong Keng Sen, 'The New Chinoiserie', *Theater* 37, no. 1 (2007): 58.

120 Charlotte Engelkes, 'The Global Soul – The Buddha Project'. Available online: http://charlotteengelkes.com/the-buddha-project/.

121 Katrin Bettina Müller, 'Das Design des Fremden' [The Design of the Strange], taz. die tageszeitung, 2 June 2003. Available online: https://taz.de/!766047/. Over the course of touring, not all seven artists were always available, and so the version Müller saw involved five rather than seven journeys.

122 MC93, 'La veuve et le lettré', Bobigny program (2013–2014): 63. In the interest of full disclosure, I should note that I worked for both French and Chinese sides of these collaborative projects in various capacities, but principally as translator and interpreter, and published a brief account of the 2014 tour as 'The Touring Canteen: Notes from the 2014 European Tour of the Quanzhou Liyuan Theatre', *CHINOPERL: Journal of Chinese Oral and Performing Literature* 34, no. 1 (2015): 46–56.

NOTES   131

123 The seminal contact here is probably the 1982 European concert tour of Tainan Nanshengshe 台南南聲社, which lasted twenty-five days and included an 'all-night concert at Radio France with simultaneous broadcast across Europe and a five-hour seminar', and was arranged by Hokkien culture and Taoism specialist Kristofer Schipper (1934–2021). Wang, 'Lessons from the Past', 169.

124 Fabienne Darge, 'Le théâtre chinois sous un autre jour' [Chinese Theatre in a Different Light], *Le Monde*, 26 June 2015. Available online: https://www.lemonde.fr/scenes/article/2015/06/29/le-theatre-chinois-sous-un-autre-jour_4663638_1654999.html.

125 Fabienne Pascaud, 'La drôle de poésie du Théâtre Liyuan' [Liyuan Theatre's Poetic Wit], *Télérama*, 22 June 2015. Available online: https://www.telerama.fr/sortir/la-drole-de-poesie-du-theatre-liyuan,127955.php.

126 Fabienne Darge, 'Mariage arrangé sur la scène franco-chinoise' [Arranged Marriage on the Sino-French Stage], *Le Monde*, 20 May 2016. Available online: https://www.lemonde.fr/scenes/article/2016/05/28/mariage-arrange-sur-la-scene-franco-chinoise_4928291_1654999.html.

127 The composition, co-commissioned with the Conservatoire, premiered at the Philharmonie de Paris in 2018. Guillaume Tion, 'Le grand projet de La Petite Mélancolie' [The Great Project of the Lesser Melancholy], *Libération*, 9 February 2018. Available online: https://www.liberation.fr/musique/2018/02/09/le-grand-projet-de-la-petite-melancolie_1628607/.

Chapter 2

1   'Weeping tunes' (*kudiao* 哭調) in *gezaixi* were also a major feature of Taiwanese theatre. It may be that reading this musical development principally as a feature of Taiwanese political history (Teri Jayne Silvio, 'Drag Melodrama/Feminine Public Sphere/Folk Television: "Local Opera" and Identity in Taiwan' [PhD diss., University of Chicago, 1998], 132–5) does not sufficiently account for the influence of similar tendency

132 NOTES

to melancholy as a dominant theatrical aesthetic in other and older Hokkien theatres.

2   Wang, 'Xu', 2.

3   Max Bohnenkamp's useful mapping of the genealogy of 'integrated art form', imported from European and Soviet theatrical modernism, points out that its allure in China emerged from 'an impression that it could provide a theoretical foundation for a new type of theatre that was consummately modern in a world-historical sense, while also helping maximize theatre's affective impact on audiences, as well as resolve the contradictions of Eastern and Western cultural identi[t]y implied by modernity's Eurocentric foundations'. Max L. Bohnenkamp, 'Neither Western Opera, Nor Old Chinese Theater', in *Intangible Heritage Embodied*, ed. Xiaomei Chen, Tarryn Li-Min Chun and Siyuan Liu (Ann Arbor: University of Michigan Press, 2021), 38. Although in principle it was originally used to invoke new, synthetic theatre, the term now seems to be invoked mostly to defend the aesthetic principles of *xiqu* as a traditional family of genres.

4   Darge, 'L'art du liyuan ne craint pas la modernité'.

5   D. Fairchild Ruggles and Helaine Silverman, 'From Tangible to Intangible Heritage', in *Intangible Heritage Embodied*, ed. Helaine Silverman and D. Fairchild Ruggles (New York: Springer, 2009), 7.

6   This is, for instance, the case in the Wang Kui 王魁 narrative, which is thought to be representative of the *nanxi* version of this narrative. Unlike in other genres, however, in which the concubine Wang has jilted wreaks revenge upon him as a ghost, in the *liyuanxi* version Wang Kui is able to appease her supernatural wrath by recognizing her virtue by building a memorial arch. Huang Wenjuan 黄文娟, 'Liyuanxi "Wang Kui" de chuantong xushi he dangdai qishi 梨園戲《王魁》的傳統敘事和當代啓示' [Traditional Narration and Contemporary Revelation in Liyuanxi's Wang Kui], *Xiqu yanjiu* 95 (2016): 126–38. By and large, the encounter with Western aesthetics generated a concern in China from the late nineteenth century that Chinese theatre did not really achieve sublimity, since tragedy was to be rated the highest of literature. This concern now seems misplaced, not least because *xiqu* was so often

NOTES 133

performed in scenes (that do not end happily) rather than as full narratives (which generally do).

7   The eminent theatre scholar Hu Ji dedicated an article to the number 'eighteen' in *xiqu*, pointing out that it has parallels in the eighteen arhats of Buddhism or the eighteen changes a girl is said to undergo in puberty. In *liyuanxi* it is not only the 'eighteen movements' that are highlighted but also the 'eighteen plays' that operate sometimes as an approximative number (e.g. important plays in repertoire) and sometimes a number simply indicating 'many'. Hu Ji 胡忌, 'Huashuo "shiba" yu xishi 話説"十八"與戲史 [On the Number 'Eighteen' and Theatre History], in *Xishi bian* 戲史辨, vol. 3, ed. Hu Ji and Luo Di (Beijing: Zhongguo xiju chubanshe, 1999), 388–90.

8   Huadong xiqu yanjiu yuan, *Huadong xiqu juzhong jieshao*, 104.

9   Wang, 'Xu', 4.

10 The most extensive treatment of *liyuanxi* role types of which I am aware is in Wu, *Liyuanxi yishu shilun*, 363–74, and the treatment here is much indebted to Wu's account.

11 Wu, *Liyuanxi yishu shilun*, 363; Sun, 'Performances of *nanxi*', 150–3.

12 Indeed, there are some historic scripts which were intended for acting or pedagogical use, and only furnish one role's lines.

13 Elizabeth Wichmann, 'Tradition and Innovation in Contemporary Beijing Opera Performance', *TDR* 34, no. 1 (1990): 146.

14 Regina Llamas, 'Retribution, Revenge, and the Ungrateful Scholar in Early Chinese Southern Drama', *Asia Major* 20, no. 2 (2007): 98.

15 Ying-fen Wang, 'The "Mosaic Structure" of Nanguan Songs: An Application of Semiotic Analysis', *Yearbook for Traditional Music* 24 (1992): 26. *Qupai* are a phenomenon across traditional *xiqu* and orchestral traditions and are sometimes also referred to in English as 'labelled tunes', 'labelled melodies' or 'tune matrices'.

16 The demonstrable antiquity of some of the *qupai* names has sometimes been produced as evidence for the history of the genre. Such affirmations should be treated with caution, since

134   NOTES

qupai names and metres have often been borrowed from earlier genres of poetry or performance.

17   Wu, *Liyuanxi yishu shilun*, 81.

18   Wang, 'The "Mosaic Structure" of *Nanguan* Songs', 25.

19   A further element, sometimes confusing to the foreign reader, is the fact that the prosodic categories have 'labels' which are usually references to a locus classicus for this *qupai*, but they are not meaningfully the 'name' of a certain piece.

20   The other prevalent form of musical organization in *xiqu* is the *banqiangti* 板腔體, although certain *xiqu* genres also mix the two of them, and the relation between the two systems is contested. See Alan R. Thrasher, *Qupai in Chinese Music: Melodic Models in Form and Practice* (New York: Routledge, 2016), in particular Chapter 8 '*Qupai* Suite Forms in *Nanguan* and Other Traditions' in which Thrasher discusses the *nanguan/nanyin* use of *qupai*, which is the foundation of *liyuanxi*'s use of the same.

21   Huadong xiqu yanjiu yuan, *Huadong xiqu juzhong jieshao*, 113.

22   Lim, 'Nanyin Musical Culture in Southern Fujian', 238–9.

23   For use of *gongche pu* in *nanyin* music in Taiwan, see Chou Chiener, 'Experience and Fieldwork: A Native Researcher's View', *Ethnomusicology* 46, no. 3 (2002): 460–2.

24   Wu, *Liyuanxi yishu shilun*.

25   There are more male characters who use them, but this practice too is diminishing.

26   Ye, *Liyuanxi shihua*, 20–1.

27   Zeng Jingping 曾静萍, 'Ba liyuanxi de jingsui hua ru xieye 把梨園戲的精髓化入血液' [Letting the Essence of Liyuanxi Flow into the Bloodstream], *Zhongguo xiqu xueyuan xuebao* 37, no. 4 (2016): 4.

Chapter 3

1   Although the practice dates from at least the Qing, the term *zhezi xi* itself seems to be no older than the mid-twentieth century (Tseng Yong-yih 曾永義, 'Lunshuo "zhezixi" 論說折子戲'

NOTES 135

[On *Zhezixi*], *Xiju yanjiu* 1 (2008): 2–4) and for *liyuanxi* is probably borrowed from analogous practices in more northern genres. It is thought that the term may arise from *kunqu*, with the folding booklets (*zhezi* 褶子) into which single scenes were copied for singing. See Wu Xinlei 吳新雷, ed., *Zhongguo Kunju da cidian* 中國崑劇大辭典 [Great Dictionary of Chinese *Kunju*] (Nanjing: Nanjing daxue chubanshe, 2002), 47.

2   Similarly, *Chen San and Wuniang* only added the female protagonist's name, Wuniang, to the title for the one-night version in the 1950s; previously it had likewise only been known by the male protagonist's name.

3   Wu, *Liyuanxi yishu shilun*, 144.

4   Contemporary or twentieth-century dress productions today are largely in the direct service of the party-state. The 2001 performance was for the eightieth anniversary of the CCP, and in 2021 as this book was being written the troupe was again preparing a political drama based on revolutionary struggle for the party's centenary.

5   The 'little theatre' (*xiao juchang* 小劇場) movement initially developed in Taiwan in response to Western theories of theatre, including Grotowski's 'poor theatre'. From there it became a shorthand for modest, fringe-like, stripped-down types of theatre in the PRC as well. The intersection of 'little theatre' and *xiqu* in both Taiwan and Mainland China has provided space to play with the technical capital of *xiqu* while leaving the constraints of repertoire. The fact that it is in an alternative space may perhaps provide an alibi for some experimentation, because it relieves the claim to be performing 'tradition'.

6   For an example of how technique was transmitted in 2015 through festival programming of a scene, 'Yitong Settles the Rice-Cake Accounts' (Yitong suan guo zhang 義童算粿賬), that had not been performed since the 1980s see Josh Stenberg, 'Repertoire Is Technique: Programming Transmission at a Xiqu Festival', *Theatre Topics* 26, no. 1 (2016): 119–20.

7   The term, which works out to 'eighteen representative repertoire pieces' is *shiba pengtou* 十八棚頭, with *peng* being the theatre shed with a raised stage (*xipeng* 戲棚) and *tou* meaning head or chief, and here referring to the most important repertoire piece on the programme.

NOTES

8   Hu, 'Huashuo "shiba" yu xishi', 51–4. The information of the repertoire, when not drawn from programmes or viewings or otherwise indicated, comes from Wu, *Liyuanxi yishu shilun*; Ye, *Liyuanxi shihua*; van der Loon, *The Classical Theatre and Art Song of South Fukien*; and accounts given by actors.

9   The story is widely performed in China but became very famous through the *huangmeixi* 黃梅戲 version which achieved success at the same 1954 Eastern China Opera Observation and Performance Convention where *Chen San and Wuniang* brought *liyuanxi* to national prominence. Idema, *The Metamorphosis of Tianxian pei*.

10   Siyuan Liu, 'The Great Traditional/Modern Divide of Regional Chinese Theatrical Genres in the 1950s', *Theatre Journal* 70, no. 2 (2018): 161; Wilt L. Idema, *Passion, Poverty and Travel: Traditional Hakka Songs and Ballads* (Hackensack: World Century Publishing Corporation, 2015), 191–215; 381–402. Idema (191–2) notes the similarities with *The Lute* and other stories of students forced into bigamy, with the notable distinction that the story of the second wife's cruelty to the first is particular to the Gao Wenju narrative.

11   Van der Loon heard audiorecordings of it issued by the Art-Tune Co. COL-3022/3024. Van der Loon, *The Classical Theatre and Art Song of South Fukien*, 71–6.

12   The southern drama version is canonical, but not attached to any author. For a translation and an introduction to the *zaju* northern drama version, attributed to Guan Hanqing 關漢卿, see Stephen H. West and Wilt L. Idema, eds and trans., *Monks, Bandits, Lovers, and Immortals: Eleven Early Chinese Plays* (Indianapolis: Hackett Publishing Company, 2010), 70–105.

13   Van der Loon, *The Classical Theatre and Art Song of South Fukien*, 58–60.

14   Yiheng Zhao, 'Subculture as Moral Paradox: A Study of the Texts of the *White Rabbit* Play', in *The River Fans Out*, ed. Yiheng Zhao (Springer: Singapore, 2020), 53–80.

15   Van der Loon, *The Classical Theatre and Art Song of South Fukien*, 69–71; Wang Renjie 王仁傑, '"Zhu Bian" Chongyan ganyan 《朱弁》重演感言' [Feelings upon Reviving 'Zhu Bian'], *Fujian yishu* 1 (2010): 66.

NOTES

137

16   It is also popular in ballads and in the visual arts. Scarlett Jang, 'Form, Content, and Audience: A Common Theme in Painting and Woodblock-printed Books of the Ming Dynasty', *Ars Orientalis* 27 (1997): 1–26.

17   S-C. Kevin Tsai, 'Ritual and Gender in the "Tale of Li Wa"', *Chinese Literature: Essays, Articles, Reviews* 26 (2004): 99–127; Glen Dudbridge, *The Tale of Li Wa* (London: Ithaca Press, 1983).

18   The name Zhao Zhennü 趙真女 is outside of *liyuanxi* more often written 趙貞女.

19   While the narrative is persuasively cited as an example of the ungrateful scholar being recovered for respectability by later literati (Llamas 2007), the *liyuanxi* fragments do not seem either to be an ungrateful scholar narrative or a literati rewrite.

20   Llamas, 'Retribution, Revenge, and the Ungrateful Scholar', 82.

21   Llamas, 'Retribution, Revenge, and the Ungrateful Scholar', 79–81.

22   Wang An-chi 王安祈, 'Youguan liyuanxi Wang Kui juben yanjiu de ji dian buchong he yiwen 有關梨園戲王魁劇本研究的幾點補充和疑問' [A Few Notes and Questions about Wang Kui Manuscripts in Liyuanxi], *Minsu quyi* 76 (1992): 59–71; Zeng Jinzheng 曾金錚, 'Liyuanxi ji ge gu jiaoben de tansuo – "Wang Kui" "Wang Shipeng" "Guo Hua" "Lü Mengzheng" 梨園戲幾個古腳本的探索——《王魁》《王十朋》《郭華》《呂蒙正》' [Exploring Some Old Liyuanxi Scripts – *Wang Kui, Wang Shipeng, Guo Hua, Lü Mengzheng*], in *Nanxi Lunji*, ed. Fujian xiqu yanjiusuo (Beijing: Zhongguo xiju chubanshe, 1988), 235–40.

23   Huang, 'Liyuanxi "Wang Kui" de chuantong xushi he dangdai qishi', 126–38.

24   Jing Shen, 'Ethics and Theater: The Staging of Jingchai ji in Bimuyu', *Ming Studies* 2008, no. 1 (2008): 70–1.

25   Cai, 'Ming chuanqi "Lizhi ji" yanbian chutan', 33.

26   These are now in the Piet van der Loon collections at the Bodleian Library.

27   Taylor, 'Lychees and Mirrors', 167. Chen San is actually Chen Boqing 陳伯卿 and in some song collections this name is given

for the narrative. Being the third of his family he is known as Chen San 陳三 and he adopts this name when he indentures himself in Wuniang's household to be close to his beloved.

28 This film was produced by Shanghai Tianma productions, and is easily found on streaming services such as YouTube or Bilibili.

29 As early as the twelfth century, the Lantern Festival was recorded as both a major festivity in the region and the occasion for performance. Lin, Zheng and Liu, *Fujian xishi lu*, 16–17.

30 Guotong Li, *Migrating Fujianese: Ethnic, Family, and Gender Identities in an Early Modern Maritime World* (Leiden: Brill, 2016), 131–51.

31 Claudine Lombard-Salmon, 'Aux origines de la littérature sino-malaise: un sjair publicitaire de 1886' [At the Origin of Sino-Malay Literature: An Advertising Sjair from 1886], *Archipel* 8, no. 1 (1974): 168.

32 Claudine Salmon, ed., *Literature in Malay by the Chinese of Indonesia* (Paris: Editions de la Maison des sciences de l'homme, 1981), 474–5; Claudine Salmon, 'Malay Translations of Chinese Fictions in Indonesia', in *Literary Migrations: Traditional Chinese Fiction in Asia, 17–20th Centuries*, ed. Claudine Salmon (Singapore: Institute of Southeast Asian Studies, 2013), 256, 268; John B. Kwee, 'Chinese Malay Literature of the Peranakan Chinese in Indonesia 1880–1942' (PhD diss., University of Auckland, 1978), 37; Henk Maier, 'Explosions in Semarang: Reading Malay Tales in 1895', *Bijdragen tot de Taal-, Land- en Volkenkunde* 162, no. 1 (2006): 18. The story sometimes underwent surprising alterations. Kwee notes of a 1922 printing that it includes 'a rather indecent bedroom scene, where Tan Sha not only made love with Go Nio but also with her maid' (1978, 39).

33 National interest in *liyuanxi* is generally dated to these performances. The festival was an important springboard for regional theatre beginning in 1951, until at least 1955; after that, the 'collective performances' seem to have become provincial rather than regional.

NOTES

139

34 Bai Yonghua 白勇華, 'Shiqi nian "xigai" guocheng zhong de minjian yu guojia – yi Fujian difangxi wei kaocha zhongxin' 十七年'戲改'過程中的民間與國家 – 以福建地方戲為考察中心' [The Folk and the Nation during the Seventeen-Year Opera Reform – Taking Fujian Folk Operas as Center of Investigation], (PhD diss., Fujian Normal University, 2016), 72.

35 Van der Loon, *The Classical Theatre and Art Song of South Fukien*, 17. Other theatrical versions went further: Chen San's ruse to remain in Wuniang's household – deliberately breaking a mirror he was meant to be polishing – was turned instead into an accident. The alteration seems to reflect a general effort to make sympathetic figures in *xiqu* less crafty or libidinous, but van der Loon writes that the alteration was never accepted in Quanzhou. In van der Loon's estimation, this mutilated the plot, and he deemed it as fortunate that this change, part of the plot in the 1950s, had been reverted in the versions performed in the 1980s.

36 The troupe actually was founded in 1953, but since the Lantern Festival falls at the beginning of the year, and because the Shanghai performances of 1954 were also seminal for the troupe's contemporary fortunes, the anniversary festivities were held in 2014.

37 Ye, *Liyuanxi shihua*, 167. The film also had an impact on the stage performance. For instance, an orchestral overture written for the film is now used for the stage as well, and is moreover popular as a concert piece.

38 The script had circulated in the 1950s, but was first published in a 1992 book called *Lingering Notes of Southern Drama* (*Nanxi yixiang* 南戲遺響). Wu Jieqiu 吳捷秋, 'Quanqiang nanxi de Song Yuan guben – Liyuanxi gu chao can ben "Zhu Wen Zougui" xiao shu 泉腔南戲的宋元孤本 – 梨園戲古抄殘本《朱文走鬼》校述' [The Only Copy of a Song or Yuan Dynasty Script in Quanzhou-melody Southern Drama – A Fragment from an Old Liyuanxi Manuscript], in *Nanxi yixiang* 南戲遺響 [Lingering Notes of Southern Drama], ed. Quanzhou difang xiqu yanjiu she (Beijing: Zhongguo xiju chubanshe, 1991), 5–55; Piet van der Loon, 'Chu Wen: A Play for the Shadow Theatre', in *Occasional Papers of the European*

Association of Chinese Studies (Paris: European Association of Chinese Studies, 1979), 75; Wu, *Liyuanxi yishu shilun*, 206–15.

39 Van der Loon, 'Chu Wen: A Play for the Shadow Theatre'.

40 Maggie Greene notes that in fact ghost operas in various forms continued to be performed despite official dissatisfaction, and that the sharp turn against performing rather than adapting ghost plays did not occur until 1963; Maggie Greene, *Resisting Spirits: Drama Reform and Cultural Transformation in the People's Republic of China* (Ann Arbor: University of Michigan Press, 2019).

41 Van der Loon, *The Classical Theatre and Art Song of South Fukien*, 84.

42 The *kunqu* version of the story is perhaps the best known. Josh Stenberg, 'Staging Female-initiated Divorce: The Zhu Maichen Story in Twentieth-century Drama from Opprobrium through Approbation', *Nan Nü* 16, no. 2 (2014): 308–40; Josh Stenberg, 'An Annotated Translation of Zhang Jiqing's Lecture on Playing Cui-shi in Chimeng (The Mad Dream): A Sample Lecture from Kunqu baizhong, Dashi shuoxi (One Hundred Pieces of Kunqu, Master Performers Talk about Their Scenes)', *CHINOPERL: Journal of Chinese Oral and Performing Literature* 35, no. 2 (2016): 153–75.

43 Fu Jin 傅謹, 'Ruhe rang Zhu Maichen gushi you jiaoyu yiyi 如何讓朱買臣故事有教育意義' [How to Give the Story of Zhu Maichen Educational Meaning], *Bolan qunshu* 博覽群書 3 (2006): 49.

44 This version first appears in *zaju, Zhu Taishou fengxue yuqian ji* 朱太守風雪漁樵記 [Prefect Zhu, the Woodcutter and the Fisherman, amidst the Wind and Snow] collected in *Yuanqu xuan* 元曲選 [*Selected Yuan plays*; 1616] by Zang Maoxun 臧懋循 (1550–1620). 'Zhu's wife (who is called Jade Immortal 玉天仙 in this play) divorces her husband not out of her own frustration with his poverty, but at her father's command. His intention is to motivate his son-in-law to advance his scholarly career, which has apparently stalled through the excessive comfort of domesticity'. See Stenberg, 'Staging Female-initiated Divorce', 319–20.

NOTES

141

45 For instance, Zhu Maichen is addressed as *jieyuan* 解元, a Song practice, rather than *xiucai* 秀才, as he would be in later versions. Lin Rensheng, whose unpublished notes Wu quotes, adduces a number of other pieces of evidence, including from Quanzhou proverbs, that might suggest the play had an early appearance in the area. Unlike some other pieces of *liyuanxi*, repertoire, however, there is no direct textual evidence linking it to Song or Yuan dynasty *nanxi* plays. See Wu, *Liyuanxi yishu shilun*, 29.

46 This is the matter for a different line of research altogether, but it is worth noting that such *zuibaixi*, featuring little or no music, closely resemble spoken theatre. One might further consider whether the hard distinction between *xiqu* and spoken theatre, according to which China developed spoken theatre in reaction to Western and Japanese models, is in fact partially a product of the fact that core genres of comparison (*jingju*, *kunqu*, Cantonese opera) have no such scenes. Certainly, several traditional *liyuanxi* scenes would essentially seem to be 'spoken theatre' rather than music-drama or dance-drama.

47 This version, dictated to Lin Rensheng, was collected in volume 4 of the *Collectanea* (2000, 1–53). In recent years the troupe has preferred to revive older repertoire from the pre-edited manuscripts, which retain more profanity as well as repetition. The 2016 version thus bypasses Lin Rensheng's own 1962 version, which to some degree adapted the plot to the necessities of party ideology (for instance by giving sympathetic characters more proletarian backgrounds). See Wu, *Liyuanxi yishu shilun*, 230. A much shorter Qing manuscript fragment exists for the *dan* role, reproduced in the *Collectanea* (54–63) alongside some related *nnayin* lyrics.

48 The passages from *Zhu Maichen* are adapted from the author's surtitles for the FPLET's performance of the show.

49 Zeng Jingping, personal communication, 26 September 2019.

50 Shen Qifeng 沈起風, *Xie duo* 諧鐸 [Words of Humour from an Ancient Bell] (Changsha: Yuelu shushe, 1986), 45–7.

51 Since 1997 the prize has been called the Cao Yu Theatre Prize.

52 Yu Qiufen 余秋芬, 'Wen tian 問天' [Ask the Heavens], *Taiwan da baike jin shu*, 9 September 1998. Available online: https://nrch.culture.tw/twpedia.aspx?id=12541.

53 Wang Renjie 王仁傑, 'Wo xie *Jiefuyin* 我寫節婦吟' [How I Wrote *The Chaste Woman's Lament*], in *Fujian sheng youxiu juzuo xuan (1979–1989)* 福建優秀劇作選 (1979–1989) [Selected Outstanding Dramas from Fujian Province (1979–1989)], ed. Liu Shijin, Liu Baochuan and Zhang Peng (Fuzhou: Haixia wenyi chubanshe, 1990), 481. The haste in which the first draft was composed may go some way towards explaining why Wang, after over fifteen years of successful performance, felt that a (shorter, more compact) revision was called for (that version premiered in 2006). Both scripts remain in repertoire, but the revision was chosen for its most recent performances, before and during the troupe's successful 2015 visit to France.

54 Wang Renjie 王仁傑, *Sanweizhai jugao (xiudingben)*, 44.

55 One way of positing these stages is given by the anthropologist Everett Zhang, who considers the subject of romantic love to have re-emerged in the 1980s and the awakening of female desire in the 1990s. Perhaps the fact that the female desire which produces tragedy in *The Chaste Woman's Lament* (1987) but comedy in *Scholar Dong and Madam Li* (1993) represents the progress of acceptance of female desire. Everett Yuehong Zhang, 'China's Sexual Revolution', in *Deep China: The Moral Life of the Person*, ed. Arthur Kleinman, Yunxiang Yan, Jing Jun, Sing Lee, Everett Zhang, Pan Tianshu, Fei Wu and Jinhua Guo (Berkeley: University of California Press, 2011), 91–126.

56 Jun Chen and Shouhua Qi, 'Tragedy, No Tragedy, and Tragedy with Chinese Characteristics? One Hundred Years of Debate with a "Happy Ending"', *The Cambridge Quarterly* 49, no. 1 (2020): 55–71.

57 Darge, 'L'art du liyuan ne craint pas la modernité'.

58 Dai Guanqing 戴冠青, 'Wang Renjie juzuo nüxing xingxiang jiedu 王仁傑劇作女性形象解讀' [An Explanation of Female Figures in Wang Renjie's Dreams], *Quanzhou shifan xueyuan xuebao* 22, no. 1 (2004): 71.

NOTES

59 None of the thirty canonical works of *xiqu* drama, according to modern Mainland anthologies of drama, is by a woman, and only three women feature among the ninety-nine authors dealt with under the category of '*xiqu* literature' in the *Chinese Encyclopaedia*. Li Xianglin 李祥林, 'Zuojia xingbie yu xiqu chuangzuo' 作家性別與戲曲創作' [Author Gender and Xiqu Creation], *Yishu baijia* 2 (2003): 64.

60 The story did not have a pre-existing *liyuanxi* version, and is best known in its *jingju* version. For an account of Wang An-chi also experimenting with this text, see Daphne Lei, *Alternative Chinese Opera in the Age of Globalization: Performing Zero* (New York: Palgrave Macmillan, 2011), 41–6; Josh Stenberg, 'Conservative Experiments: Women's Rewritings of *The Imperial Stele Pavilion* in the Twenty-first Century', *Contemporary Theatre Review* 31, no. 3 (2021): 323–39.

61 Wang Renjie's influence is perhaps noticeable here in the willingness to knowingly employ anachronism – a historical Meng Yuehua would have no opportunity to live decently outside of the marital structure defined for her – in order to make a contemporary point.

Conclusions

1 Fu Jin 傅謹, 'Wei shenme shi Wang Renjie? Wei shenme shi liyuanxi? Weishenme shi Quanzhou? 為什麼是王仁傑?為什麼是梨園戲?為什麼是泉州?' [Why Wang Renjie? Why Liyuanxi? Why Quanzhou?], in *Qing xi cangsheng shizhi chuantong* 情系蒼生矢志傳統 [Ties of Love Bind the People to Tradition], ed. Fujian sheng liyuanxi chuancheng zhongxin, Quanzhou shi xiju yanjiusuo and Wang Renjie xiansheng qinshu (Quanzhou: FPLET, 2021), 58.

2 Joshua Goldstein, *Drama Kings: Players and Publics in the Re-Creation of Peking Opera, 1870–1937* (Berkeley: University of California Press, 2007), 46.

NOTES

3 Ashley Thorpe, 'Transforming Tradition: Performances of Jingju ("Beijing Opera") in the UK', *Theatre Research International* 36, no. 1 (2011): 33.

4 Emily E. Wilcox, 'Dynamic Inheritance: Representative Works and the Authoring of Tradition in Chinese Dance', *Journal of Folklore Research* 55, no. 1 (2018): 77–111.

BIBLIOGRAPHY

Bai Yonghua 白勇華. 'Shiqi nian "xigai" guocheng zhong de minjian yu guojia – yi Fujian difangxi wei kaocha zhongxin' 十七年'戲改'過程中的民間與國家—以福建地方戲為考察中心' [The Folk and the Nation during the Seventeen-year Opera Reform – Taking Fujian Folk Operas as Center of Investigation]. PhD diss., Fujian Normal University, 2016.

Bilingual Theatre Programme. 'Fujian Liyuan Opera Troupe – People's Republic of China – Philippine Performance Tour 1986/Zhongguo Fujian Liyuanxi Shiyan Jutuan – Fangfei yanchu tekan 中國福建梨園戲實驗劇團—訪菲演出特刊' [China's Fujian Province Liyuanxi Experimental Theatre – Philippines Tour Special Issue]. Fujian Province Liyuanxi Experimental Theatre Archives.

Bohnenkamp, Max L. 'Neither Western Opera, Nor Old Chinese Theater'. In *Intangible Heritage Embodied*, edited by Xiaomei Chen, Tarryn Li-Min Chun and Siyuan Liu, 34–60. Ann Arbor: University of Michigan Press, 2021.

Cai Tiemin 蔡鐵民. 'Ming chuanqi "Lizhi ji" yanbian chutan – Jian tan nanxi zai Fujian de yixiang 明傳奇《荔支記》演變初探 — 兼談南戲在福建的遺響' [Preliminary Thoughts on the Development of the Ming Chuanqi Script The Tale of the Lychee – Also on the Echoes of Nanxi in Fujian]. *Xiamen daxue xuebao* (zhexue shehui kexue ban) 3 (1979): 31–48.

Chang, Chia-Lan. 'Family Matters: Women's Negotiation with Confucian Family Ethics in Qing and Republican China'. PhD diss., University of Southern California, 2007.

Chang, Dongshin. 'Performing Traditions and Diasporic Efforts: The Kunqu Society and Little Pear Garden Collective'. In *Asian Canadian Theatre*, edited by Nina Lee Aquino and Ric Knowles, 49–58. Toronto: Playwrights Canada Press, 2011.

Chang, Huei-Yuan Belinda. 'A Theatre of Taiwaneseness: Politics, Ideologies, and Gezaixi'. *TDR* 41, no. 2 (1997): 111–29.

Charlotte, Engelkes. 'The Global Soul – The Buddha Project'. Available online: http://charlotteengelkes.com/the-buddha-project/.

BIBLIOGRAPHY

Chen, Jun and Shouhua Qi. 'Tragedy, No Tragedy, and Tragedy with Chinese Characteristics? One Hundred Years of Debate with a "Happy Ending"'. *The Cambridge Quarterly* 49, no. 1 (2020): 55–71.

Chen, Liana. *Staging for the Emperors: A History of Qing Court Theatre, 1683–1923*. Amherst: Cambria Press, 2021.

Chen, Ruitong 陳瑞統, ed. *Quanzhou mu'ou yishu* 泉州木偶藝術 [Quanzhou Puppet Arts]. Xiamen: Lu Jiang chubanshe, 1986.

Chen, Xiaomei, Tarryn Li-Min Chun and Siyuan Liu. *Rethinking Chinese Socialist Theaters of Reform: Performance Practice and Debate in the Mao Era*. Ann Arbor: University of Michigan Press, 2021.

Chia, Caroline. 'Gezai xi in Singapore: Oral Transmission, Improvisation and Dependence on "Fixed Texts"'. *CHINOPERL: Journal of Chinese Oral and Performing Literature* 37, no. 1 (2018): 1–41.

Chia, Caroline. *Hokkien Theatre across the Seas*. Singapore: Springer, 2019.

Chia, Caroline. 'A Preliminary Study of Kaoka 高甲 Playscripts in the Philippines'. In *Sinophone Southeast Asia: Sinitic Voices across the Southern Seas*, edited by Tom Hoogervorst and Caroline Chia, 185–209. Leiden: Brill, 2021.

Chiener, Chou. 'Experience and Fieldwork: A Native Researcher's View'. *Ethnomusicology* 46, no. 3 (2002): 456–86.

Chin, James K. 'Merchants, Envoys, Brokers and Pirates: Hokkien Connections in Pre-modern Maritime Asia'. In *Offshore Asia*, edited by Fujita Kayoko, Momoki Shiro and Anthony Reid, 53–75. Singapore: Institute of Southeast Asian Studies, 2013.

Chu Renhuo 褚人獲. *Sui Tang yanyi* 隋唐演義 [Romance of Sui and Tang Dynasties], 1695. Available online: https://ctext.org/wiki.pl ?if=en&chapter=823084&remap=gb.

Clark, Hugh R. *Community, Trade, and Networks: Southern Fujian Province from the Third to the Thirteenth Century*. Cambridge: Cambridge University Press, 2002.

Cultural Heritage Department of Taichung City. 'Zhongyao chuantong biaoyan yishu – nanguan xiqu – baocun zhe Lin Wu Suxia 重要傳統表演藝術-南管戲曲-保存者林吳素霞' [An Important Traditional Art – Nanguan xiqu – Culture-bearer Lin Wu Su-hsia]. *Cultural Heritage Department of Taichung City*, 8 January 2020. Available online: https://www.tchac.taichung. gov.tw/historybuilding?uid=38&pid=126.

BIBLIOGRAPHY

Dai Bufan 戴不凡. 'Di er ge Su Wu – Liyuanxi "Zhu bian lengshan ji" guan hou 第二個蘇武——梨園戲《朱弁冷山記》觀後' [A Second Su Wu – The Liyuan Play *Zhu Bian on the Cold Mountain*]. *Xiju bao* (1959): 22.

Dai Guanqing 戴冠青. 'Wang Renjie juzuo nüxing xingxiang jiedu 王仁傑劇作女性形象解讀' [An Explanation of Female Figures in Wang Renjie's Dramatic Work]. *Quanzhou shifan xueyuan xuebao* 22, no. 1 (2004): 70–3.

Darge, Fabienne. 'L'art du liyuan ne craint pas la modernité' [Liyuan's Art Is Not Afraid of the Modern]. *Le Monde*, 5 June 2014. Available online: https://www.lemonde.fr/culture/article/2014/06/05/l-art-du-liyuan-ne-craint-pas-la-modernite_4432320_3246.html.

Darge, Fabienne. 'Le théâtre chinois sous un autre jour' [Chinese Theatre in a Different Light]. *Le Monde*, 26 June 2015. Available online: https://www.lemonde.fr/scenes/article/2015/06/29/le-theatre-chinois-sous-un-autre-jour_4663638_1654999.html.

Darge, Fabienne. 'Mariage arrangé sur la scène franco-chinoise' [Arranged Marriage on the Sino-French Stage]. *Le Monde*, 20 May 2016. Available online: https://www.lemonde.fr/scenes/article/2016/05/28/mariage-arrange-sur-la-scene-franco-chinoise_4928291_1654999.html.

Ding, Picus Sizhi. *Southern Min (Hokkien) as a Migrating Language: A Comparative Study of Language Shift and Maintenance across National Borders*. Berlin: Springer, 2015.

Dudbridge, Glen. *The Tale of Li Wa*. London: Ithaca Press, 1983.

Fu Jin 傅謹. 'Ruhe rang Zhu Maichen gushi you jiaoyu yiyi 如何讓朱買臣故事有教育意義' [How to Give the Story of Zhu Maichen Educational Meaning]. *Bolan qunshu* 3 (2006): 49–55.

Fu Jin 傅謹. 'Wei shenme shi Wang Renjie? Wei shenme shi liyuanxi? Weishenme shi Quanzhou? 為什麼是王仁傑?為什麼是梨園戲?為什麼是泉州?' [Why Wang Renjie? Why Liyuanxi? Why Quanzhou?]. In *Qing xi cangsheng shizhi chuantong* 情系蒼生矢志傳統 [Ties of Love Bind the People to Tradition], edited by Fujian sheng liyuanxi chuancheng zhongxin, Quanzhou shi xiju yanjiusuo and Wang Renjie xiansheng qinshu, 58–61. Quanzhou: FPLET, 2021.

Fujian sheng difangzhi bianzuan weiyuanhui 福建省地方志編纂委員會 [Compilation Committee of the Fujian Province Gazetteer]. 'Duiwai wenhua jiaoliu 對外文化交流' [International Cultural Exchange]. In *Fujian sheng zhi: Wenhua yishu zhi*

BIBLIOGRAPHY

福建省志:文化藝術志 [Culture and Arts Gazetteer for Fujian Province], edited by Fujian sheng difangzhi bianzuan weiyuanhui, 612–48. Fuzhou: Fujian renmin chubanshe, 2008.

Fushiki, Kaori. 'Nanyin and the Singaporean Culture: The Creation of Intangible Cultural Heritage in Singapore and Intergenerational Contrasts'. In *Transglobal Sounds: Music, Youth and Migration*, edited by João Sardinha and Ricardo Campos, 93–112. London: Bloomsbury, 2016.

Fushiki, Kaori and Robin Ruizendaal, eds. *Potehi: Glove Puppet Theatre in Southeast Asia and Taiwan*. Taipei: Taiyuan Publishing, 2016.

Goldman, Andrea S. 'The Nun Who Wouldn't Be: Representations of Female Desire in Two Performance Genres of "Si Fan"'. *Late Imperial China* 22, no. 1 (2001): 71–138.

Goldstein, Joshua. *Drama Kings: Players and Publics in the Re-Creation of Peking Opera, 1870–1937*. Berkeley: University of California Press, 2007.

Greene, Maggie. *Resisting Spirits: Drama Reform and Cultural Transformation in the People's Republic of China*. Ann Arbor: University of Michigan Press, 2019.

Guy, Nancy A. 'Peking Opera as "National Opera" in Taiwan: What's in a Name?'. *Asian Theatre Journal* 12, no. 1 (1995): 85–103.

Guy, Nancy. *Peking Opera and Politics in Taiwan*. Champaign: University of Illinois Press, 2005.

Harrell, Stevan. 'From Xiedou to Yijun, the Decline of Ethnicity in Northern Taiwan, 1885–1895'. *Late Imperial China* 11, no. 1 (1990): 99–127.

Hong Jingyi 洪靜儀. 'Wu Suxia qi jiao xi wutai yanchu ben yanjiu 吳素霞七腳戲舞台演出本研究' [Research on Wu Su-hsia's Qijiaoxi Stage Art]. PhD diss., National Taipei University, 2011.

Hong Weizhu 洪惟助. '1963 nian Taiwan qizixi peixunban shimo jiyi yingxiang 1963 年台灣七子戲培訓班始末及其影響 [All about the 1963 Taiwanese Child Actor Training Cohort and Its Influence]. In *Haixia liang'an liyuanxi xueshu yantaohui lunwenji* 海峽兩岸梨園戲學術研討會論文集 [Cross-strait Liyuanxi Research Conference Essay Collection], edited by Tseng Yong-yih, 3–17. Taipei: Guoli Zhongzheng wenhu zhongxin, 1998.

Hsiang Ta 向達. 'Yingya suozhi – ji Niujin suo cang de wenshu 瀛涯瑣志–記牛津所藏的中文書' [Trivial Records from the

Ocean's Shores – On the Chinese Books Held in Oxford], *Guoli Peiping tushuguan guankan* X/5 (1936): 9–44.

Hsieh, Hsiao-Mei. 'Across the Strait: History, Performance and Gezaixi in China and Taiwan'. PhD diss., Northwestern University, 2008.

Hu Ji 胡忌. 'Huashuo "shiba" yu xishi 話説"十八"與戲史' [On the Number 'Eighteen' and Theatre History]. In *Xishi bian* 戲史辨 [Theatre History Debates], vol. 3, edited by Hu Ji and Luo Di, 41–67. Beijing: Zhongguo xiju chubanshe, 1999.

Huadong xiqu yanjiu yuan 華東戲曲研究院, ed. *Huadong xiqu juzhong jieshao* 1 華東戲曲劇種 介紹 1 [Introduction to Theatre Genres of Eastern China, vol. 1]. Shanghai: Xin wenyi chubanshe, 1955.

Huang Chaosong 黃朝松. 'Liang'an liyuanxi chuanxi jihua zhi xiankuang yu weilai zhanwang 兩岸梨園戲傳習計畫之現況與未來展望' [Present Situation and Future Developments of the Passing-on program for 'Liyuan' Opera on Both Sides of the Strait]. In *Chuantong yishu yantao hui: Lunwen ji* 傳統藝術研討會:論文集, edited by Guoli chuantong yishu zhongxin choubei chu, 53–84. Yilan: Guoli chuantong yishu zhongxin choubei chu, 1998.

Huang Qiongfen 黃瓊芬. 'Zeng Jingping: Rang xin linian hua wei fei yichuan cheng xin liliang 曾靜萍:讓新理念化為非遺傳承新力量' [Zeng Jingping: Let New Conceptualizing Become the New Strength of Intangible Culture Transmission]. *Dongnan wang*, 14 March 2021. Available online: http://fjnews.fjsen.com/2021-03/14/content_30668767.htm

Huang Wenjuan 黃文娟. 'Liyuanxi "Wang Kui" de chuantong xushi he dangdai qishi 梨園戲《王魁》的傳統敘事和當代啓示' [Traditional Narration and Contemporary Revelation in Liyuanxi's Wang Kui]. *Xiqu yanjiu* 95 (2016): 126–38.

Huang Wenjuan 黃文娟. 'Xigai shiqi de "Chen San Wuniang" 戲改時期的《陳三五娘》' [*Chen San and Wuniang* During Opera Reform]. *Fujian yishu* 5 (2015): 32–6.

Hunter Gordon, Kim. 'Contesting Traditional Luzi ("Choreographic Paths"): A Performance-Based Study of Kunqu'. PhD diss., University of London, 2016.

Idema, Wilt L. *The Metamorphosis of Tianxian pei: Local Opera under the Revolution (1949–1956)*. Hong Kong: The Chinese University of Hong Kong Press, 2015.

BIBLIOGRAPHY

Idema, Wilt L. *Passion, Poverty and Travel: Traditional Hakka Songs and Ballads*. Hackensack: World Century Publishing Corporation, 2015.

Idema, Wilt L. 'The Emergence of Regional Opera on the National Stage'. In *A New Literary History of Modern China*, edited by David Der-wei Wang, 585–90. Cambridge: Harvard University Press, 2018.

Jang, Scarlett. 'Form, Content, and Audience: A Common Theme in Painting and Woodblock-printed Books of the Ming Dynasty'. *Ars Orientalis* 27 (1997): 1–26.

Johnson, David. 'Report on the International Conference on Chinese Southern Opera (Nanxi) and Mulian Opera: Fukien, 2/26/91–3/5/91'. *CHINOPERL: Journal of Chinese Oral and Performing Literature* 16, no. 1 (1992): 207–14.

Kang, Yin-Chen. 'The Formation of Taiwanese Classical Theatre, 1895–1937'. PhD diss., University of London, 2013.

Kwee, John B. 'Chinese Malay Literature of the Peranakan Chinese in Indonesia 1880–1942'. PhD diss., University of Auckland, 1978.

Lei, Daphne. *Alternative Chinese Opera in the Age of Globalization: Performing Zero*. New York: Palgrave Macmillan, 2011.

Leong, Wen Kam. 'Bearers of Great Riches'. *Straits Times*, 25 September 2010.

Li, Guotong. *Migrating Fujianese: Ethnic, Family, and Gender Identities in an Early Modern Maritime World*. Leiden: Brill, 2016.

Li Xianglin 李祥林. 'Zuojia xingbie yu xiqu chuangzuo 作家性別與戲曲創作' [Author Gender and Xiqu Creation]. *Yishu baijia* 2 (2003): 64–70.

Lian Heng 連橫. *Taiwan tongshi* 台湾通史 [A General History of Taiwan], edited by Lian Yatang. Taipei: Taiwan yinhang jingji yanjiusuo, 1985.

Lianhe zaobao 聯合早報. 'Dunhuang xianzi xiafan lai – Fujian liyuanxi jin ci yi jia 敦煌仙子下凡來—福建梨園戲僅此一家' [Immortals of Dunhuang Come Down to Earth – A Single Fujian Liyuanxi Troupe]. *Lianhe zaobao*, 23 October 1991, 50.

Liao Yuning 廖于潭. 'Jiangzicui juchang "Zhu Wen zou gui" yanyi zhi yanjiu 江子翠劇場《朱文走鬼》演藝之研究' [Research on Gang-a-tsui's performance of Zhu Wen Flees the Ghost]. PhD diss., National Taiwan Normal University, 2011.

BIBLIOGRAPHY

151

Lien, Chinfa. 'Interface of Modality and the tit[4] 得 Constructions in Southern Min: A Case Study of Their Developments from Earlier Southern Min in the Ming and Qing to Modern Taiwanese Southern Min'. *Language and Linguistics* 12, no. 4 (2011): 723–52.

Lien, Chinfa and Alain Peyraube, eds. *Diachronic Perspectives and Synchronic Variation in Southern Min*. New York: Routledge, 2020.

Lim, Cloris Sau-Ping. 'Nanyin Musical Culture in Southern Fujian, China: Adaptation and Continuity'. PhD diss., University of London, 2014.

Lin Qingxi 林慶熙, Zheng Qingshui 鄭淸水 and Liu Xiangru 劉湘如, comps. *Fujian xi shilu* 福建戲史錄 [Historical Records of Theatre in Fujian]. Fuzhou: Fujian renmin chubanshe, 1983.

Lin Ruiwu 林瑞武. 'Shi xi Zeng Jingping de biaoyan yishu 試析曾靜萍的表演藝術' [An Analysis of Zeng Jingping's Art as a Performer]. *Fujian xiju* 5 (1998): 9–10.

Liu Nianzi 劉念茲. *Nanxi xin zheng* 南戲新證 [New Evidential Interpretation of Southern Drama]. Beijing: Zhonghua shuju, 1986.

Liu, Siyuan. 'Theatre Reform as Censorship: Censoring Traditional Theatre in China in the Early 1950s'. *Theatre Journal* 61, no. 3 (2009): 387–406.

Liu, Siyuan. 'The Great Traditional/Modern Divide of Regional Chinese Theatrical Genres in the 1950s'. *Theatre Journal* 70, no. 2 (2018): 153–72.

Liusha 流沙. *Mingdai nanxi shengqiang yuanliu kao bian* 明代南戲聲腔源流考辨 [Research on the Sources of Ming Dynasty Southern Drama's Vocal Music]. Taipei: Caituan faren Shi Hezheng minsu wenhua jijinhui, 1999.

Llamas, Regina. 'Retribution, Revenge, and the Ungrateful Scholar in Early Chinese Southern Drama'. *Asia Major* 20, no. 2 (2007): 75–101.

Lombard-Salmon, Claudine. 'Aux origines de la littérature sino-malaise: un sjair publicitaire de 1886' [At the Origin of Sino-Malay Literature: An Advertising Sjair from 1886]. *Archipel* 8, no. 1 (1974): 155–86.

Lu Ang 盧昂. 'Cong Liyuanxi "Dong Sheng yu Li Shi" tan qi 從梨園戲《董生與李氏》談起' [Talking about Liyuan, Starting from Scholar Dong and Madam Li]. In *Fanbenkaixin: Wang Renjie juzuo yanjiu lunwenxuan* 返本開新:王仁傑劇作研究論文選 [Returning to the Roots, Putting Out New Shoots: A Collection of Essays on Wang Renjie's Dramatic Works], edited by Xue Ruolin, Liu Zhen and Fan Biyun, 250–60. Beijing: Wenhua yishu chubanshe, 2012.

Lü Xiaoping 呂效平. '*Dong Sheng yu Li Shi*: Wang Renjie he ta de *Dong Sheng yu Li shi* 《董生與李氏》:王仁杰和他的《董生與李氏》' [*Scholar Dong and Madam Li*: Wang Renjie and His *Scholar Dong and Madam Li*]. In *Fanbenkaixin: Wang Renjie juzuo yanjiu lunwenxuan* 返本開新:王仁傑劇作研究論文選 [Returning to the Roots, Putting out New Shoots: A Collection of Essays on Wang Renjie's Dramatic Works], edited by Xue Ruolin, Liu Zhen, and Fan Biyun, 292–9. Beijing: Wenhua yishu chubanshe, 2012.

Luo, Liang. 'The Experimental and the Popular in Chinese Socialist Theater of the 1950s'. In *Rethinking Chinese Socialist Theaters of Reform: Performance, Practice, and Debate in the Mao Era*, edited by Xiaomei Chen, Tarryn Li-Min Chun and Siyuan Liu, 135–61. Ann Arbor: University of Michigan Press, 2021.

Mackerras, Colin. *Chinese Drama: A Historical Survey*. Beijing: New World Press, 1990.

Mackerras, Colin. 'Peking Opera before the Twentieth Century'. *Comparative Drama* 28, no. 1 (1994): 19–42.

Maier, Henk. 'Explosions in Semarang: Reading Malay Tales in 1895'. *Bijdragen tot de Taal-, Land- en Volkenkunde* 162, no. 1 (2006): 1–34.

MC93. 'La veuve et le lettré'. Theatre program for MC93 2013–2014: 62–3.

Ministry of Culture (Republic of China, Taiwan). 'Nanguanxi yiren 南管戲藝人' [Artists of the Nanguan Stage]. Available online: https://learning.moc.gov.tw/course/2266cd64-0b4a-4f7d-93f8-b27f99d08add/content/ar/02-1/data/downloads/02-1.pdf.

Müller, Katrin Bettina. 'Das Design des Fremden' [The Design of the Strange]. *taz: die tageszeitung*, 2 June 2003. Available online: https://taz.de/!766047/.

Ong Keng, Sen. 'The New Chinoiserie'. *Theater* 37, no. 1 (2007): 55–68.

Ouyang Xiu 歐陽修 and Song Qi 宋祁. *Xin Tangshu* 新唐書 [New Book of Tang]. Beijing: Zhonghua shuju, 1975 [1060]), zhi 12.12.

BIBLIOGRAPHY

Pan Rongyang 潘榮陽. 'Ming Qing Min-Tai diqu Lei Haiqing xinyang xingsheng tan wei 明清閩台地區雷海青信仰興盛探微' [Brief Exploration of the Rise of the Cult of Lei Haiqing in Ming and Qing Fujian and Taiwan]. *Zhongguo Daojiao* 2 (2006): 37–9.

Pascaud, Fabienne. 'La drôle de poésie du Théâtre Liyuan' [Liyuan Theatre's Poetic Wit]. *Télérama*, 22 June 2015. Available online: https://www.telerama.fr/sortir/la-drole-de-poesie-du-theatre-liyuan,127955.php.

Pearson, Richard, Li Min and Li Guo. 'Quanzhou Archaeology: A Brief Review'. *International Journal of Historical Archaeology* 6 (2002): 23–59.

Polo, Marco. *The Travels of Marco Polo*. Annotated and edited by Henri Cordier, translated by Henry Yule. London: John Murray, 2018.

Qian Chenxiang 錢陳翔. 'Cong "Taiwan Han Tang Yuefu" kan nanyin guyue de xin fazhan 從"台灣漢唐樂府"看南音古樂的新發展' [Seeing the New Development of Ancient Southern Music from Taiwan Han-tang Yuefu]. *Yinyue tansuo* 4 (2011): 31–4.

Qian Nanyang 錢南揚, ed. *Song Yuan xiwen jiyi* 宋元戲文輯佚 [Collected Song and Yuan Dynasty Nanxi Fragments]. Shanghai: Shanghai gudian wenxue chubanshe, 1956.

Quanzhou difang xiqu yanjiu she 泉州地方戲曲研究社. *Quanzhou chuantong xiqu congshu* 泉州傳統戲曲叢書 [Quanzhou Traditional Xiqu Collectanea]. Beijing: Zhongguo xiju chubanshe, 2000.

Rebull, Anne Elizabeth. 'Theaters of Reform and Remediation: Xiqu (Chinese Opera) in the Mid-twentieth Century'. PhD diss., University of Chicago, 2017.

Rolandsen, Unn Målfrid. *Leisure and Power in Urban China: Everyday Life in a Chinese City*. London: Routledge, 2011.

Ruggles, D. Fairchild and Helaine Silverman. 'From Tangible to Intangible Heritage'. In *Intangible Heritage Embodied*, edited by Helaine Silverman and D. Fairchild Ruggles, 1–14. New York: Springer, 2009.

Ruizendaal, Robin. *Marionette Theatre in Quanzhou*. Boston: Brill, 2006.

Salmon, Claudine, ed. *Literature in Malay by the Chinese of Indonesia*. Paris: Editions de la Maison des sciences de l'homme, 1981.

BIBLIOGRAPHY

Salmon, Claudine. 'Malay Translations of Chinese Fictions in Indonesia'. In *Literary Migrations: Traditional Chinese Fiction in Asia, 17–20th Centuries*, edited by Claudine Salmon, 248–76. Singapore: Institute of Southeast Asian Studies, 2013.

Schipper, Kristofer 施舟人. 'The Maritime Silk Road and Nanyin Music' '海上絲綢之路'與南音. In *Quanzhou gang yu haishang sichou zhi lu guoji xueshu yantaohui lunwenji* 泉州港與海上絲綢之路國際學術研討會論文集 [Collected Essays from the Academic Conference on Quanzhou Harbour and the Maritime Silk Harbour], edited by Zhongguo Hanghai Xuehui, 70–85. Beijing: Zhongguo shehui kexue chubanshe, 2002.

Shen, Huifen. 'Engendering Chinese Migration History: "Left-behind Wives of the Nanyang Migrants" in Quanzhou before and after the Pacific War'. PhD diss., National University of Singapore, 2006.

Shen, Jing. 'Ethics and Theater: The Staging of Jingchai ji in Bimuyu'. *Ming Studies* 2008, no. 1 (2008): 62–101.

Shen Qifeng 沈起鳳. *Xie duo* 諧鐸 [Words of Humour from an Ancient Bell]. Changsha: Yuelu shushe, 1986.

Shi Ruilou 施瑞樓. 'Huainian zhongyao minzu yishu yishi Li Xiangshi xiansheng – Ji Li shi ersan shi 懷念重要民族藝術藝師李祥石先生 – 記李師二三事' [In Memory of the Important Ethnic Artist, Mister Li Xiangshi – Remembering Two or Three Things about Mister Li]. In *Li Xiangshi yishi nanguanxi juben – koushu chuanlu* 李祥石藝師南管戲劇本—口述傳錄 [The Li Xiangshi Nanguan Theatre Script – Oral Records], edited by Shi Ruilou, 7–28. Taipei: National Taiwan Arts Education Center, 2004.

Shih Cheng-xing 施政昕. 'Lun Han Tang Yuefu de "Luoshen fu" bian yan celüe: Yi changci anpai, yuandian yingyong yu yinyue sheji wei zhongxin 論漢唐樂府的《洛神賦》編演策略:以場次安排、原典應用與音樂設計為中心' [Arrangement and Performance Strategies of 'The Lyric for Lo River Goddess' by Han-Tang Yuefu Music Ensemble: Session Organization, Literary Allusion and Music Design]. *Zhongguo wenxue yanjiu* 49 (2020): 41–74.

Silvio, Teri Jayne. 'Drag Melodrama/Feminine Public Sphere/Folk Television: "Local Opera" and Identity in Taiwan'. PhD diss., University of Chicago, 1998.

Sommier, Patrick. 'L'Art des nations: Travailler dans un théâtre en Chine et en Russie' [L'Art des nations: Working in a Theatre in China and in Russia]. *KROUM* (18–28 January 2018): 8–9.

Stenberg, Josh. 'Staging Female-initiated Divorce: The Zhu Maichen Story in Twentieth-century Drama from Opprobrium through Approbation'. *Nan Nü* 16, no. 2 (2014): 308–40.

Stenberg, Josh. 'Performance Review: Nanguan Meets Modern Chinese Poetry: Wang Xinxin's Nanguan shiyi (Nanguan/Poetic meaning) Taiwan Tour, May 2015'. *CHINOPERL: Journal of Chinese Oral and Performing Literature* 34, no. 2 (2015): 179–81.

Stenberg, Josh. 'The Touring Canteen: Notes from the 2014 European Tour of the Quanzhou Liyuan Theatre'. *CHINOPERL: Journal of Chinese Oral and Performing Literature* 34, no. 1 (2015): 46–56.

Stenberg, Josh, trans. 'An Annotated Translation of Zhang Jiqing's Lecture on Playing Cui-shi in Chimeng (The Mad Dream): A Sample Lecture from Kunqu baizhong, Dashi shuoxi' [One Hundred Pieces of Kunqu, Master Performers Talk about Their Scenes]. *CHINOPERL: Journal of Chinese Oral and Performing Literature* 35, no. 2 (2016): 153–75.

Stenberg, Josh. 'Repertoire Is Technique: Programming Transmission at a Xiqu Festival'. *Theatre Topics* 26, no. 1 (2016): 117–29.

Stenberg, Josh. 'Conservative Experiments: Women's Rewritings of the Imperial Stele Pavilion in the Twenty-First Century'. *Contemporary Theatre Review* 31, no. 3 (2021): 323–39.

Stenberg, Josh and Jason J.P. Cai. 'Mostly Young Women with Quite Traditional Tastes: Empirical Evidence for National Contemporary Audiences of Xiqu'. *Theatre Journal* 69, no. 1 (2017): 43–59.

Stenberg, Josh and Zhang Jingjing. 'Scholar Dong and Madam Li Step out: Are There National Audiences for Chinese Traditional Regional Theatre?'. *Theatre Research International* 40, no. 1 (2015): 50–66.

Su Yanshi 蘇彥石. 'Fujian sheng de zuijia nü yanyuan Zeng Jingping 福建省的最佳女演員曾靜萍' [Zeng Jingping, the Best Actress of Fujian Province]. *Xiju bao* 5 (1988): 60.

Su Yanshi 蘇彥石. 'Qiangjiu jicheng chuangxin – Fujian sheng Liyuanxi shiyan jutuan wushi nian huigu 搶救·繼承·創新——福建省梨園戲實驗劇團五十年回顧' [Rescue, Transmit, Innovate – Looking Back on Fifty Years of the FPLET]. *Fujian yishu* 1 (2003): 44–6.

156 BIBLIOGRAPHY

Su Yingmi 蘇英蜜. 'Tan Liyuanxi de jicheng yu gaige 談梨園戲的繼承與改革' [On the Transmission and Reform of Liyuan Theatre]. *Fujian yishu* 2 (1999): 12–13.

Sun, Mei. 'Performances of *nanxi*'. *Asian Theatre Journal* 13, no. 2 (1996): 141–66.

Sun, Mei. 'The Division between "Nanxi" and "Chuanqi"'. *American Journal of Chinese Studies* 5, no. 2 (1998): 248–56.

Sun, Mei. 'Exploring the Historical Development of Nanxi, Southern Theater'. *CHINOPERL: Journal of Chinese Oral and Performing Literature* 24, no. 1 (2002): 35–65.

Tan, Marcus. 'Fabulous Review: The Global Soul: The Buddha Project by Theatreworks'. *The Flying Inkpot*, 21 June 2003. Available online: http://www.inkpotreviews.com/oldInkpot/03reviews/03revglobsoulbuddproj.html

Tan, Shzr Ee. 'Unequal Cosmopolitanisms: Staging Singaporean Nanyin in and beyond Asia'. In *Asian City Crossings: Pathways of Performance through Hong Kong and Singapore*, edited by Rossella Ferrari and Ashley Thorpe, 189–211. London: Routledge, 2021.

Taylor, Jeremy E. 'Lychees and Mirrors: Local Opera, Cinema, and Diaspora in the Chinese Cultural Cold War'. *Twentieth-Century China* 43, no. 2 (2018): 163–80.

Thorpe, Ashley. 'Transforming Tradition: Performances of Jingju ("Beijing Opera") in the UK'. *Theatre Research International* 36, no. 1 (2011): 33–46.

Thrasher, Alan R. *Qupai in Chinese Music: Melodic Models in Form and Practice*. New York: Routledge, 2016.

Tion, Guillaume. 'Le grand projet de La Petite Mélancolie' [The Great Project of the Lesser Melancholy]. *Libération*, 9 February 2018. Available online: https://www.liberation.fr/musique/2018/02/09/le-grand-projet-de-la-petite-melancolie_1628607/.

Tsai, S-C. Kevin. 'Ritual and Gender in the "Tale of Li Wa"'. *Chinese Literature: Essays, Articles, Reviews* 26 (2004): 99–127.

Tseng Yong-yih 曾永義. 'Lunshuo "zhezixi" 論說折子戲' [On Zhezixi]. *Xiju yanjiu* 1 (2008): 1–82.

Van der Loon, Piet. 'Chu Wen: A Play for the Shadow Theatre'. In *Occasional Papers of the European Association of Chinese Studies*, 75–91 and i–xxxii. Paris: European Association of Chinese Studies, 1979.

BIBLIOGRAPHY

Van der Loon, Piet. *The Classical Theatre and Art Song of South Fukien: A Study of Three Ming Anthologies*. Taipei: SMC Publishing, 1992.

Wake, Christopher. 'The Great Ocean-Going Ships of Southern China in the Age of Chinese Maritime Voyaging to India, Twelfth to Fifteenth Centuries'. *International Journal of Maritime History* 9, no. 2 (1997): 51–81

Wang An-chi 王安祈. 'Youguan liyuanxi Wang Kui juben yanjiu de ji dian buchong he yiwen 有關梨園戲王魁劇本研究的幾點補充和疑問' [A Few Notes and Questions about Wang Kui Manuscripts in Liyuanxi]. *Minsu quyi* 76 (1992): 59–71.

Wang Hanmin 王漢民. *Fujian xiqu haiwai chuanbo yanjiu* 福建戲曲海外傳播研究 [Research on Fujian Xiqu's Performance Abroad]. Beijing: Zhongguo shehui kexue chubanshe, 2011.

Wang Renjie 王仁傑. 'Wo xie Jiefuyin 我寫"節婦吟"' [How I Wrote *The Chaste Woman's Lament*]. In *Fujian sheng youxiu juzuo xuan (1979–1989)* 福建省優秀劇作選 (1979–1989) [Selected Outstanding Dramas from Fujian Province (1979–1989)], edited by Liu Shijin, Liu Baochuan and Zhang Peng, 480–547. Fuzhou: Haixia wenyi chubanshe, 1990.

Wang Renjie 王仁傑. 'Liyuan shide jiushidiao fanzuo xinshengchang duanchang – xiju xinde zatan 梨園拾得舊時調翻作新聲唱斷腸—習劇心得雜談' [Collecting Old Melodies in a Pear Garden, Turning them into Heart-Rending New Voices: Random Discoveries from a Life in Theatre]. *Juben* 12 (1997): 2–3.

Wang Renjie 王仁傑. '"Zhu Bian" Chongyan ganyan 《朱弁》重演感言' [Feelings upon Reviving 'Zhu Bian']. *Fujian yishu* 1 (2010): 66.

Wang Renjie 王仁傑. *Sanweizhai jugao (xiudingben)* 三畏齋劇稿(修訂本)[Manuscripts from the Three Reverences (revised edition)]. Beijing: Zhongguo xiju chubanshe, 2012.

Wang Renjie 王仁傑. 'Xu 序' [Introduction]. In *Liyuanxi shihua* 梨園戲史話 [Notes on Liyuanxi History], edited by Ye Xiaomei, 1–5. Beijing: Shehui kexue wenxian chubanshe, 2015.

Wang Renjie 王仁傑. 'Gu, gu, gu 孤, 古, 固' [Solitary, Ancient, Stubborn]. In *Qing xi cangsheng shizhi chuantong* 情系蒼生矢志傳統 [Ties of Love Bind the People to Tradition], edited by Fujian sheng liyuanxi chuancheng zhongxin, Quanzhou shi xiju yanjiusuo and Wang Renjie xiansheng qinshu, 109–19. Quanzhou: FPLET, 2021.

BIBLIOGRAPHY

Wang Renjie 王仁傑 and Tan Huafu 譚華孚. 'Xiqu wenhua de fanben yu kaixin: Yin Chen Zhongzi er qi de duihua 戲曲文化的返本與開新:因《陳仲子》而起的對話' [Return to Roots and New Shoots in Xiqu Culture: A Dialogue Beginning from Chen Zhongzi]. *Fujian xiju* (1991): 34–6.

Wang Wei 王偉. 'Fujian xiqu gaige yu gujin lijing qingyuan 福建戲曲改革與古今荔鏡情緣' [Fujianese Opera Reform and Versions of the Lychees and the Mirror through the Ages]. *Yiyuan* 6 (2016): 11–17.

Wang, Yibo. 'Liyuan Opera Lizhiji: New Materials, Stories and Insights'. PhD diss., University of Edinburgh, 2019.

Wang, Ying-fen. 'Lessons from the Past: Nanguan/Nanyin and the Preservation of Intangible Cultural Heritage in Taiwan'. In *Music as Intangible Cultural Heritage: Policy, Ideology, and Practice in the Preservation of East Asian Traditions*, edited by Keith Howard, 161–80. Farnham: Ashgate, 2012.

Wang, Ying-fen. 'The "Mosaic Structure" of Nanguan Songs: An Application of Semiotic Analysis'. *Yearbook for Traditional Music* 24 (1992): 24–51.

Wang, Ying-fen. 'Tune Identity and Compositional Process in Zhongbei Songs: A Semiotic Analysis of Nanguan Vocal Music'. PhD diss., University of Pittsburgh, 1992.

West, Stephen H. and Wilt L. Idema, eds. and trans. *Monks, Bandits, Lovers, and Immortals: Eleven Early Chinese Plays*. Indianapolis: Hackett Publishing Company, 2010.

West, Stephen H. and Wilt L. Idema, eds. *The Orphan of Zhao and Other Yuan Plays: The Earliest Known Versions*. New York: Columbia University Press, 2014.

Wichmann, Elizabeth. 'Tradition and Innovation in Contemporary Beijing Opera Performance'. *TDR* 34, no. 1 (1990): 146–78.

Wichmann-Walczak, Elizabeth. 'Remembering the Past in the Shanghai Jingju Company's King Lear.' In *Shakespeare in Hollywood, Asia, and Cyberspace*, edited by Alexander Cheng-Yuan Huang and Charles Stanley Ross, 183–94. West Lafayette: Purdue University Press, 2009.

Wilcox, Emily E. 'Dynamic Inheritance: Representative Works and the Authoring of Tradition in Chinese Dance'. *Journal of Folklore Research* 55, no. 1 (2018): 77–111.

Wu Jieqiu 吳捷秋. *Liyuanxi yishu shilun* 梨園戲藝術史論 [A History of Liyuanxi Artistry]. Beijing: Zhongguo xiju chubanshe, 1996.

BIBLIOGRAPHY

Wu Jieqiu 吳捷秋. 'Quanqiang nanxi de Song Yuan guben – Liyuanxi gu chao can ben "Zhu Wen Zougui" xiao shu 泉腔南戲的宋元孤本—梨園戲古抄殘本《朱文走鬼》校述' [The Only Copy of a Song or Yuan Dynasty Script in Quanzhou-melody Southern Drama – A Fragment from an Old Liyuanxi Manuscript]. In *Nanxi yixiang*, edited by Quanzhou difang xiqu yanjiu she, 5–55. Beijing: Zhongguo xiju chubanshe, 1991.

Wu Xinlei 吳新雷, ed. *Zhongguo Kunju da cidian* 中國崑劇大辭典 [Great Dictionary of Chinese Kunju]. Nanjing: Nanjing daxue chubanshe, 2002.

Xie Zichou 謝子丑. 'Shusheng shi shou Han jia jie – Liyuanxi 'Zhu Bian' Zhong de aiguo qijie 書生誓守漢家節—梨園戲《朱弁》中的愛國氣節' [A Scholar Keeping Han Integrity – Patriotic Integrity in Liyuanxi's Zhu Bian]. *Fujian yishu* 1 (2010): 67–8.

Xu, Peng. 'The Music Teacher: The Professionalization of Singing and the Development of Erotic Vocal Style During Late Ming China.' *Harvard Journal of Asiatic Studies* 75, no. 2 (2015): 259–97.

Xu, Ya-xian. *Sounds from the Other Side: The Operatic Interaction between Colonial Taiwan and China during the Early Twentieth Century, translated by Jo-hsuan Wang*. Taipei: SMC Publishing, 2013.

Xue Ruolin 薛若琳, Liu Zhen 劉禎 and Fan Biyun 範碧雲, eds. *Fanbenkaixin: Wang Renjie juzuo yanjiu lunwenxuan* 返本開新:王仁傑劇作研究論文選 [Returning to the Roots, Putting out New Shoots: A Collection of Essays on Wang Renjie's Dramatic Works]. Beijing: Wenhua yishu chubanshe, 2012.

Yan Zihe 顏梓和, comp. 'Gezaixi ban "Shuang zhu feng" de caifang ziliao 歌仔戲班"雙珠鳳"的採訪資料' [Interview Materials of the 'Double-Pearl Double-Phoenix Troupe']. In *Gezaixi ziliao huibian* 歌仔戲資料匯編 [Gezaixi Resource Compendium], edited by Chen Geng, Zeng Xuewen and Wu Anhui, 126–7. Beijing: Guangming ribao chubanshe, 1997.

Ye Xiaomei 葉曉梅. *Liyuanxi shihua* 梨園戲史話 [Notes on Liyuanxi History]. Beijing: Shehui kexue wenxian chubanshe, 2015.

Yu Qiufen 余秋芬. 'Wen tian 問天' [Ask the Heavens]. *Taiwan da baike jin shu*, 9 September 1998. Available online: https://nrch.culture.tw/twpedia.aspx?id=12541.

Yu Weimin 俞為民. 'Song Yuan "Si da nanxi" zai liyuanxi zhong de liuchuan yu bianyi 宋元"四大南戲"在梨園戲中的流傳與變異' [The Alterations in the Liyuan Opera Adaptations of 'The Four Great Nanxi Plays']. *Wenhua yishu yanjiu* 12, no. 1 (2019): 64–76.

Zeitlin, Judith T. 'Music and Performance in Hong Sheng's *Palace of Lasting Life*'. In *Trauma and Transcendence in Early Qing Literature*, edited by Wilt L. Idema, Wai-yee Li and Ellen Widmer, 454–87. Leiden: Brill, 2006.

Zeng Jingping 曾静萍. 'Ba liyuanxi de jingsui hua ru xieye 把梨園戲的精髓化入血液' [Letting the Essence of Liyuanxi Flow into the Bloodstream]. *Zhongguo xiqu xueyuan xuebao* 37, no. 4 (2016): 1–6.

Zeng Jinzheng 曾金錚. 'Liyuanxi ji ge gu jiaoben de tansuo – "Wang Kui" "Wang Shipeng" "Guo Hua" "Lü Mengzheng" 梨園戲幾個古腳本的探索──《王魁》《王十朋》《郭華》《呂蒙正》' [Exploring some Old Liyuanxi Scripts – Wang Kui, Wang Shipeng, Guo Hua, Lü Mengzheng]. In *Nanxi Lunji*, edited by Fujian xiqu yanjiusuo, 235–40. Beijing: Zhongguo xiju chubanshe, 1988.

Zhang Aiding 張艾丁. 'Liyuanxi "Chen San Wuniang" 梨園戲"陳三五娘"' [The Liyuanxi Version of *Chen San and Wuniang*]. *Xiju bao* 9 (1955): 14–16.

Zhang, Beiyu. *Chinese Theatre Troupes in Southeast Asia: Touring Diaspora, 1900s–1970s*. London: Routledge, 2021.

Zhang, Beiyu. 'Travelling with Chinese Theatre-Troupes: A "Performative Turn" in Sino-Southeast Asian Interactions'. *Asian Theatre Journal* 38, no. 1 (2021): 191–217.

Zhang, Everett Yuehong. 'China's Sexual Revolution'. In *Deep China: The Moral Life of the Person*, edited by Arthur Kleinman, Yunxiang Yan, Jing Jun, Sing Lee, Everett Zhang, Pan Tianshu, Fei Wu and Jinhua Guo, 91–126. Berkeley: University of California Press, 2011.

Zhao, Yiheng. 'Subculture as Moral Paradox: A Study of the Texts of the White Rabbit Play'. In *The River Fans out*, edited by Yiheng Zhao, 53–80. Springer: Singapore, 2020.

Zheng Guoquan 鄭國權. 'Huoxia qu, chuanxialai 活下去, 傳下來' [Live on, Pass on]. In *Nanxi yixiang*, edited by Quanzhou difang xiqu yanjiu she, 251–64. Beijing: Zhongguo xiju chubanshe, 1991.

BIBLIOGRAPHY

Zheng Guoquan 鄭國權. "'Li jing ji" san bian《荔鏡記》三辨' [Three Arguments about the Story of the Lychees and the Mirror]. In *Xishi bian* 戲史辨 [Theatre History Debates], vol. 4, edited by Hu Ji and Luo Di, 298–346. Beijing: Zhongguo xiju chubanshe, 2004.

Zhongguo xiqu yanjiuyuan 中國戲曲研究院, ed. *Zhongguo gudian xiqu lunzhu jicheng di san ji* 中國古典戲曲論著集成第三集 [Classical Chinese Xiqu Treatises, vol. 3]. Beijing: Zhongguo xiju chubanshe, 1959.

Zhu Jingying 朱景英. *Haidong zhaji* 海東札記 [Notebooks of Haidong] juan 3, 1773. Available online: https://ctext.org/wiki.pl?if=en&chapter=368490.

Zhuang Changjiang 莊長江. *Quanzhou xi ban* 泉州戲班 [Theatre Troupes of Quanzhou]. Fuzhou: Fujian renmin chubanshe, 2006.

INDEX

Account of Southern Drama
  (*Nanci xulu* 南詞敘錄)
  18, 80
aesthetics 1–2, 4, 9, 37–8,
  58–62, 132 n.6
Aquino, Corazon 48
Ask the Heavens (*Wen tian* 問
  天) 95
Attahir, Benjamin 57
audiences 1–2, 8, 37, 41, 44,
  48–9, 52, 54, 58–9, 61,
  70–1, 73, 75, 77–8,
  86, 91–4, 100–2, 105,
  127 n.95

Bai Shuxian 白淑賢 127 n.94
banqiangti 板腔體 134 n.20
Beijing 7, 32, 34, 56, 81, 89, 92,
  96, 102
Belt and Road Initiative 7
Bobigny program MC-93
  130 n.122
Boen Sing Hoo 86
Bohnenkamp, Max 132 n.3
boy actors. *See* child actors/
  performance
budaixi/potehi 布袋戲 (glove
  puppet theatre) 9, 50
Buddha/Buddhism/Buddhist
  53, 55, 76, 113 n.22,
  133 n.7
butoh dance, Japanese 52

Cai Bojie 蔡伯喈 82–3,
  116–17 n.9
Cai Qingping 蔡清平 90
Cai Xiuying 蔡秀英 72–3, 77
Cai Yazhi 蔡婭治 46
Cai Youben 蔡尤本 25, 30,
  34, 80, 87, 112 n.19,
  122 n.56
Cantonese language 8,
  113 n.23
Cao Yu Theatre Prize
  141 n.51
chaoju 潮劇 35, 86
Chaozhou 17, 19–20, 23, 35,
  86, 118 n.18
Chen Boqing 陳伯卿. *See* Chen
  San 陳三
Chen Chun 陳淳 21
Chen Jiajian 陳家薦 72–3
Chen Maoren 陳懋仁 22
Chen Mei-O 陳美娥 49, 52–3
Chen San 陳三 (character)
  19–20, 23, 46, 85, 87–88,
  137 n.27
Chen San and Wuniang (*Chen
  San Wuniang* 陳三五娘)
  10, 19–20, 23, 31, 35,
  48–9, 52, 57, 66, 72–3,
  80, 84–8, 99, 112 n.19,
  135 n.2, 136 n.9
Chen Songlu 陳嵩祿 48
Cheng Yanqiu 程硯秋 54

INDEX

163

child actors/performance 14–15, 22–3, 25, 63–4, 79, 85, 120 n.36, 121 n.48

chuanqi 傳奇 (legend) dramas 17

Cold Mountain (*Lengshan ji* 冷山記) 32, 81

The Correct Beginnings of the Nine Modes (*Jiugong zhengshi* 九宮正始) 18

Covid-19 pandemic 42

crab-hand (*pangxie shou* 螃蟹手) 62

cross-cultural theatre 54–5

Cultural Revolution (1966–1976) 2, 32–5, 37–8, 40, 46

dachengxi 打城戲 theatre 9

danwei (單位 work-unit) system 41, 43–4

dan 旦 (female role type) 27, 37, 46, 62, 64–5, 71, 141 n.47

 great dan (dadan 大旦) 65

 second dan (*erjiadan* 二架旦) 65

 small dan (*xiaodan* 小旦) 65–6

Daoguang period (1821–1850) 88–9

diaspora. *See* Hokkien, diaspora

The Dilapidated Kiln (*Poyao ji* 破窯記) 81

disciples of the Pear Garden (*liyuan zidi* 梨園子弟) 113 n.27, 115 n.39

Dong Yong 董永 79

Double Pearl Double Phoenix (Shuangzhu feng 雙珠鳳) troupe 25

Dunhuang caves 110 n.3

eagle-talon hand (*ying zhao shou* 鷹爪手) 62

Eastern China Opera Observation and Performance Convention (Huadong qu xiqu guanmo yanchu dahui 華東區戲曲觀摩演出大會) 31, 87

economy/economic development 7–8, 24, 35, 37, 39, 41, 44, 57

education, theatre 15, 24, 40, 42–3, 53

eighteen techniques (*shiba kemu* 十八科母) 61, 78–9

The Embroidered Robe (*Xiuru ji* 繡襦記) 77

'The Emperor's Disciples of the Pear Garden' 113 n.27

The Fairy Couple (*Tianxian pei* 天仙配) 79

Fifteen Strings of Cash (*Shiwu guan* 十五貫) 34, 48, 124 n.70

folding booklets 褶子 (*zhezi*) 135 n.1

France 53, 56, 142 n.53

Fujian Province Liyuanxi Experimental Theatre, FPLET (Fujian sheng liyuanxi shiyan jutuan 福建省梨園戲實驗劇團) 4,

164 INDEX

10, 13, 16, 20, 23, 30–2, 34–5, 38, 41, 43–4, 46–7, 52–4, 56, 65, 69–71, 89–90, 99, 124 n.68

Fujian Province Quanzhou Art School, FPQAS (Fujiansheng Quanzhou yishu xuexiao 福建省泉州藝術學校) 40, 42, 69, 126 n.85

Fujian xi shilu 福建戲史錄, Historical Records of Theatre in Fujian (Lin, Zheng and Liu) 115 n.1, 119 n.29

Fu Jin 傅謹 107

Fuzhou 111 n.12

Galin-Paris-Chevé system 69

Gang-a-Tsui ensemble (Jiangzicui juchang 江子翠劇場) 53, 129 n.112

gaojiaxi 高甲戲 9, 47, 51

Gao Wenju 高文舉 79, 136 n.10

gauze headgear sheng (*shamao sheng* 紗帽生) 65

gender 24, 45–7, 64–5, 101–6, 108, 127 n.95

gezaixi 歌仔戲 9, 25, 47, 50, 86, 112 n.19, 127 n.95, 131 n.1

ginger root hand (*jiangmu shou* 薑母手) 62

The Golden Hairpin (Jinchai ji 金釵記) 83

Goldstein, Joshua 108

Gong Wanli 龔萬里 99

Gong Xianhe 龔顯鶴 24

greater Pear Garden repertoire (*da liyuan*) 14–15, 23,

26. *See also* lesser Pear Garden repertoire; Pear Garden

'The Great Melancholy' (Da men 大悶) 10, 55, 72–5, 86

Greene, Maggie 140 n.40

Guan Hanqing 關漢卿 136 n.12

Guangdong 8, 86

Guangzhou 5, 7, 56

gunmen 滾門 (tune families) 66

Guo Hua 郭華/*Rouge (Yanzhi ji* 胭脂記) 80

guzheng 69

Han-Tang Yuefu 漢唐樂府 group 52

hangdang 行當 (role types) 63–6

hanging hand gait (*chuishou xing* 垂手行) 62

Hangzhou 15

Haphe Academy (Hehe yiyuan 合和藝苑) 51–2

He Qiaoyuan 何喬遠 21–2

He Shumin 何淑敏 26–8, 82–3, 91, 122 n.56

heart-press gait (*an xin xing* 按心行) 62–3

Hokkien 4, 21–2, 24, 41–2, 50–1, 81

dialects 8, 21

diaspora 4, 8–10, 17, 24–5, 47–9, 86

migration of speakers to Southeast Asia 8

and Quanzhou (*see* Quanzhou)

Taiwanese Hokkien 8, 50

INDEX

165

Hong Kong 34, 41, 102, 110 n.1, 126 n.87
  Art-Tune Co. (Huawen zhipian chang 華文製片廠) 80
  Hong Kong Chinese Opera Festival (2019) 92
Hsiang Ta (Xiang Da 向達) 118 n.17
Hu Ji 胡忌 133 n.7
Huang Chun'an 黃春安 49
Huang Wenjuan 黃文娟 132 n.6
huangmeixi 黃梅戲 136 n.9
Humorous Notes from an Ancient Bell (*Xie duo* 諧鐸) 95

Idema, Wilt L. 136 n.10
  The Metamorphosis of Tianxian pei: Local Opera under the Revolution (*1949–1956*) 123 n.59
income/salary of performers 40–3
The Imperial Stele Pavilion (*Yubei ting* 御碑亭) 46, 57, 71, 92, 102–6
Institutional History of the Tang (*Tang huiyao* 唐會要) 11
integrated art form (*zonghe yishu* 綜合藝術) 60, 132 n.3

Jao Tsung-I 饒宗頤 118 n.17
Japan/Japanese 16, 18–19, 22, 24–5, 34, 54, 141 n.46
  butoh dance 52
jia 家 70
Jiang Shilong 蔣世隆 80

Jiangxi province 7, 23
jinghu 69
jingju 京劇 4, 23, 50, 56, 62, 67, 70, 95, 102–3, 106–7, 109, 114 n.29, 122 n.54, 141 n.46, 143 n.61
Jinjiang 7, 32
Jinjiang County Great Liyuan Experimental Theatre (Jinjiang xian da liyuan shiyan jutuan 晉江縣大梨園實驗劇團) 29–30
Jinjiang District Liyuanxi Theatre (Jinjiang qu liyuanxi jutuan xiju jutuan 晉江區梨園戲劇劇團) 33–4
Jinjiang Region Arts School (Jinjiang diqu yishu xuexiao 晉江地區藝術學校). *See* Fujian Province Quanzhou Art School
Jinliansheng Gaojia Troupe 金蓮升高甲劇團 35

Kang, Yin-Chen 112 n.19
Killing a Dog (*Shagou ji* 殺狗記) 116 n.9
Kominka movement (1937–1945) 25
kunqu 崑曲 16–17, 34, 41, 48, 67, 70, 92, 103, 107, 114 n.29, 115 n.1, 124 n.70, 127 n.95, 135 n.1, 140 n.42, 141 n.46
Kuomintang (KMT) 50
Kurata Junnosuke 倉田淳之助 118 n.17
Kwee, John B. 138 n.32

INDEX

lam yin (Cantonese 南音) 113 n.23

Lantern Festival 35, 80, 85–6, 88, 138 n.29, 138 n.36

laodan (老旦 elderly role type) 66

laoxi (老戲 old theatre) 14, 22

Laurel, Salvador H. 48

Lavaudant, Georges 57

Lei Haiqing 雷海青 12–13, 114 n.35

Lemoine, Jean René 56

Lescot, David 56

lesser Pear Garden repertoire (*xiao liyuan*) 14–15, 22–3, 25, 50–1, 63, 66, 79, 81, 121 n.48. *See also* greater Pear Garden repertoire; Pear Garden

Lien Heng 連橫 (1878–1936) 22

Li Hong 李紅 63

Li Xiangshi 李祥石 50–1

Li Yaxian 李亞仙 48, 77, 82, 90

Lijing ji 荔鏡記 (*The Story of the Lychees and the Mirror*) 19, 24

Lin Feng 林楓 22

Lin Jianpu 林劍僕 96

Lin Luanzhen 林鸞珍 121 n.46

Lin Qiuhan 林秋韓 63

Lin Rensheng 林任生 31, 77, 79, 81–2, 87, 89, 123 n.64, 141 n.45, 141 n.47

Lingering Notes of Southern Drama (*Nanxi yixiang* 南戲遺響) 139 n.38

linguistic system 8, 20

little theatre (*xiao juchang* 小劇場) movement 78, 135 n.5

Liu Nianzi 劉念茲 18

Liu Wenlong 劉文龍 83

Liu Zhiyuan 劉智遠 21, 81, 116 n.9

Liyuan Classical Theatre 44–5, 58

liyuanxi 梨園戲

and Cultural Revolution 32–3

diasporic 47–9

and gender 45–7

international network of 54–7

make-up and costumes 46, 58, 70–1, 73, 109

in modern era 24–9

music (*see* music/musicians/ musical instruments)

origin of 11–14, 16

post-Mao (*see* post-Mao era)

and PRC 4, 29–32, 54

records of 21–3

recruitment of actors 32, 38–45

role types 63–7, 133 n.10 (*see also* seven-role system)

techniques 37 (*see also* eighteen techniques)

tendencies of 14–15, 21, 78–9

Lizhi ji 荔枝記 (*The Story of the Lychee Branch*) 19

Lu Ang 盧昂 102

Lü Mengzheng 呂蒙正 21, 81

Lü Tongliu 呂同六 130 n.117

INDEX

167

Lü Xiaoping 呂效平 37
Lu Xun 魯迅 33
The Lute (*Pipa ji* 琵琶記) 82–3, 116 n.9, 136 n.10

Mackerras, Colin, *Chinese Drama: A Historical Survey* 116 n.4
Malaysia 8–9
Mandarin 7–9, 21, 23, 42, 69–70, 107
Manila 6, 9, 25, 47
  liyuanxi in 50–1
  Manila Chinese community 48–9
Mantian chun 漫天春 (*All-embracing Spring*) 19–20, 63, 80–1, 88
Mao Weitao 茅威濤 127 n.94
Maritime Silk Road 7
maritime trade 5–6
MC93 (Maison de la Culture 93) theatre 55–6, 130 n.122
Mei Lanfang 梅蘭芳 54, 118 n.17
Ming dynasty (1368–1644) 1, 12, 17–20, 30, 65, 81
Minnan 6, 20, 111 n.12
miscellany drama (*zaju* 雜劇). *See zaju* 雜劇
Moon-praying Pavilion (Baiyue ting 拜月亭) 80
Müller, Katrin Bettina 130 n.121
Museum of Traditional Nan Bei Music and Theatre (Nanbeiguan yinyue xiqu guan 南北管音樂戲曲館) 51

music/musicians/musical instruments 1, 15, 26, 30, 33, 49, 52–5, 60, 66–70
  aizai 噯仔 68
  decorative notes (*zhuangshi yin* 裝飾音) 69
  dongxiao 洞簫 67
  erxian 二弦 68
  gongche pu 工尺譜 69, 134 n.23
  jianpu 簡譜 69
  music culture of Fujian 54
  nangu (南鼓)/southern drum 68
  nanpa 南琶 67–8
  percussion instruments 59, 66, 68–9, 73
  pinxiao 品簫 67
  pu 譜 67
  qupai 曲牌 (labelled tunes/labelled melodies) 66–7, 73, 133 nn.15–16, 134 nn.19–20
  qu 曲 66–7
  recitation 69–70
  sanxian 三弦 67
  sung portions 66
  suona 嗩吶 68–9
  tempo 10, 68
  tune families 66
  tuqiang 土腔 22
  weeping tunes (*kudiao* 哭調) 131 n.1
  xiao 73
  yajiaogu 壓脚鼓 68
  zhi 指 67

Nan'an 32, 124 n.68
nanguan 南管 (southern pipes)/*nanyin* 南音 10,

30, 49–50, 52–3, 56,
66–7, 69, 81, 84, 86,
113 n.23, 134 n.20
nanguanxi 南管戲 (southern
pipes theatre) 30, 50–1,
53–4
Nanjing 81, 92
nanqu 南曲 (southern melodies)
113 n.23
nanxi 南戲 (southern drama)
3, 17–21, 23, 30, 32,
54, 63, 65, 80–1, 83–4,
88–90, 115 n.1, 132 n.6,
141 n.45
National Stage Arts
Masterpieces Project
(Guojia wutai yishu
jingpin gongcheng 國家舞
台藝術精品工程) 102
New Book of Tang (*Xin Tangshu*
新唐書) 11, 113 n.27
New Girls' Troupe (Xin nüban
新女班) 25

old theatre (*laoxi* 老戲). *See*
greater Pear Garden
repertoire
Ong Keng Sen 130 n.119
*The Global Soul – The
Buddha Project* 55
Oppenheim, Sarah 56
Ouyang Yuqian 歐陽予倩
118 n.17

The Painted Tower (*Cailou ji* 彩
樓記) 81
Pavilion of the Moon (*Yueting ji*
月亭記) 81
Pear Garden 11–12, 15,
113 n.27, 114 n.29, 115
n.39, 126 n.81. *See also*

greater Pear Garden
repertoire; lesser Pear
Garden repertoire
Pear Garden theatre. *See
liyuanxi*
Pei Yanling 裴艷玲 127 n.94
People's Republic of China
(PRC) 2–3, 8–9, 12,
14–15, 17, 20–1, 23, 27,
29, 34, 37, 39–40, 46,
50, 52, 71, 77, 80, 89,
101, 118 n.17, 122 n.54,
124 n.70, 126 n.84,
135 n.5
cultural policy 2, 29
and Philippines 48
Philippines 47–8, 50–2
Philippine Cultural Center 47
Polo, Marco 5
poor theatre 135 n.5
post-Mao era 4, 33–9, 53–4,
62, 70, 78, 99, 101, 108,
124 n.70
prosody 3–4, 32, 37, 60, 66–70,
134 n.19
puppet theatres 6, 9, 12, 21,
50, 86
Putian 21, 111 n.12, 115 n.1
puxianxi 莆仙戲 12, 21, 115 n.1

Qian Nanyang 錢南揚 19
Qing dynasty (1644–1911) 1,
12, 17, 24, 30, 121 n.44,
134 n.1
qiziban (七子班 seven-children
ensemble) 15, 63
quanqiang 泉腔 (Quanzhou
melody) 22
Quanzhou 4, 12, 16, 19, 21–2,
24, 29, 31–3, 39, 41, 45,
53–4, 56–8, 69, 84–6,

INDEX 169

107, 112 n.16, 121 n.44, 124 n.68, 126 n.87, 139 n.35
child actors in 121 n.48
commerce/trade 6–7
and Hokkien culture and identity 5–11, 69–70
Lei Haiqing temples in 13
Marco Polo on 5
Quanzhou wreck 5
Quanzhou Traditional Xiqu Collectanea (*Quanzhou chuantong xiqu congkan* 泉州傳統戲曲叢刊) 21, 61, 77, 81, 83–4, 91, 94, 112 n.19, 117 n.9, 141 n.47
Qu Liuyi 曲六乙 102

recitation 69–70, 74
recruitment, actor 32, 38–45
revolutionary operas 2, 33, 37, 78
ripped shirt *sheng* (*poshan sheng* 破衫生) 65
ritual practices 11–14, 24, 28, 31
promotion dance (*tiaojiaguan*) 13
Romances of the Sui and Tang (*Sui Tang yanyi* 隋唐演義) 12
Ruizendaal, Robin 110 n.4
Russia 56

scenes (*zhezixi* 折子戲) 20, 31, 52, 56, 61–2, 65, 81, 83, 88, 116 n.9, 133 n.6, 135 n.1
selected scenes format 76
solo scene 65–6, 72–5, 86

talking scenes (*zuibaixi* 嘴白戲) 91
traditional 81, 141 n.46
Schipper, Kristofer 131 n.123
scripts 4, 9, 17–21, 23, 31, 34–5, 39, 51, 64, 76–9, 82–3, 89, 91, 95, 102–3, 108–9, 122 n.56, 133 n.12, 139 n.38
seven-role system 63–6
chou 丑 (clown) 26, 64, 66
dan 旦 (*see dan* 旦 (female role type))
jing 淨 (painted face) 64, 66, 71
mo 末 (older male servants) 64, 66
sheng 生 (scholar role) 37, 64–5, 71
tie 貼 (maidservants) 64, 66
wai 外 (miscellaneous) 64, 66
Shanghai 7, 31, 87
Shanghai Little Theatre Chinese Opera Festival 92
shanglu (上路 upper circuit) repertoire 14, 26, 82, 91
Shen Qifeng 沈起風 95
Shi Hongbao 施鴻保, *Fujian Notes* (閩雜記 Min zaji) 23
Shi Xiaomei 石小梅 127 n.95
shiba pengtou 十八棚頭 135 n.7
shigong 師公 (Daoist priest) 113 n.22
shigongxi 師公戲 (Daoist ritual) 113 n.22
The Shoes Left Behind (*Liuxie ji* 留鞋記) 80
'Si fan' 思凡 (Longing for the Secular Life) 20

INDEX

Silian Musical Studio (Silian yuefu 四聯樂府) 50–1
Singapore 9, 25, 49, 55
  liyuanxi in 50–4
  Peranakan culture in 6
  Siong Leng Musical Association 53
Sinophone 37, 49
Sommier, Patrick 45, 55–7
Song dynasty (960–1279) 5, 15, 81, 141 n.45
Southeast Asia 6, 8, 24, 41, 47, 53, 86, 126 n.87
  Southeast Asian Chinese 4, 7
southern drama. See nanxi 南戲 (southern drama)
Southern Fujian Experimental Troupe (Minnanxi shiyan jutuan 閩南戲實驗劇團) 30
spoken theatre 2, 24, 37–8, 141 n.46
The Story of the Pearl (Zhenzhu ji 珍珠記) 79
The Story of the White Rabbit (Baitu ji 白兔記) 81
Su Ou 蘇鷗 85
Su Qin 蘇秦 21, 26, 82
Su Wushui 蘇烏水 85
Su Yanshi 蘇彥石 34, 39, 77, 83
Sun Rong 孫榮 116 n.9
Sy, Henry 施至成 111 n.13

Tainan Nanshengshe 台南南聲社 131 n.123
Taipei National University of the Arts (Guoli Taibei yishu daxue 國立臺北藝術大學) 52
Taiwan 4, 6, 9–10, 12, 16, 22–5, 30, 47, 49, 88,
102, 112 n.16, 122 n.54, 122 n.58
  Hokkien in 7–8, 50
  little theatre movement in 135 n.5
  liyuanxi in 50–4
  nanguanxi in 51
  Tainan 22–3, 50
talent-and-beauty narratives (caizi jiaren 才子佳人) 15
Tan Sha Go Nio 86. See also Chen San and Wuniang
Tang dynasty (618–906) 5, 16, 113 n. 28
The Thorn Hairpin (Jingchai ji 荊釵記) 84, 116 n.9
Thorpe, Ashley 109
Thrasher, Alan R. 134 n.20
Tian, Marshal (Tian 田都元帥). See Lei Haiqing
Tseng Yong-yih 曾永義 49
Twenty-four Filial Exemplars (Ershi si xiao 二十四孝) 84
'The Two Fingers Commendation' (Liangzhi tijing 兩指題旌) 95

van der Loon, Piet 16, 19, 115 n.2, 115 n.39, 118 n.18, 122 n.56
  The Classical Theatre and Art Song of South Fukien 116 n.6, 117 n.12, 118 n.20, 119 n.31, 136 n.11, 139 n.35

Wang An-chi 王安祈 95, 102, 143 n.61
Wang Hanmin 王漢民, Fujian xiqu haiwai chuanbo

INDEX

yanjiu 福建戲曲海外傳播研究 (Research on Fujian Xiqu's Performance Abroad) 121 n.47, 124 n.75

Wang Kui 王魁 83, 132 n.6

Wang Renjie 王仁傑 11, 34–7, 59–60, 62, 81, 95, 98–9, 101, 103–5, 115 n.2, 121 n.44, 123 n.64, 142 n.53, 143 n.62

    The Chaste Woman's Lament (*Jiefu yin* 節婦吟) 34–5, 38, 49, 56, 95–8, 101, 103, 142 n.55

    Chen Zhongzi 陳仲子 35, 38, 57

    Liyuanxi shihua 梨園戲史話 (Notes on Liyuanxi History) 115–16 n.2

    Lü Xiaoping on 37–8

    Maplewood Evening (*Fenglin wan* 楓林晚) 35, 78

    Scholar Dong and Madam Li (*Dongsheng yu Lishi* 董生與李氏) 35, 37, 56, 98–103, 142 n.55

Wang Shipeng 王十朋 21, 84, 116 n.9

Wang Xinxin 王欣欣 53

Wang, Yibo 20

WeChat 41

Wei-Guinot, Pascale 56

wenyi xuanchuan dui 文藝宣傳隊 (cultural propaganda team) 33

Western theatres 2–3, 37, 44, 53, 61, 65, 67

The White Hare (*Baitu ji* 白兔記) 116 n.9

Wichmann-Walczak, Elizabeth 110 n.1

Wilcox, Emily 109

women playwrights 46, 57, 71, 92, 102–6

Wu Jieqiu 吳捷秋 23, 31, 49, 122 n.56

    Liyuanxi yishu shilun 梨園戲藝術史論 (A History of Liyuanxi Artistry) 122 n.58, 133 n.10

Wu Shou-li 吳守禮 19

Wu Su-hsia 吳素霞 51–2

Xiamen 6–7, 23, 25, 35

xianan (下南 down south) repertoire 14, 26–7, 64, 67, 81–2

xiangju 薌劇 9

Xianyou county 115 n.1

Xu Maocai 許茂才 27

Xu Shuji 許書紀 29

Xu Tianxiang 許天相 73

Xu Xiang 徐祥 51

Xu Zaiquan 許在全 49

Xu Zhiren 許志仁 25–6

Xuanzong, Emperor 玄宗 11

Xue Ningdu 薛凝度 23

Yan Zihe 顏梓和 120 n.46

Yao Suqin 姚蘇秦 28

Yap, Pedro L. 48

'Yitong suan guo zhang' 義童算粿賬 (Yitong Settles the Rice-cake Accounts) 28, 135 n.6

Yongle Compendium (*Yongle dadian* 永樂大典) 80, 88

You Yubin 尤毓彬 68

172 INDEX

Yu Jian 俞儁 71
Yu Yonghe 郁永河 22
Yuan dynasty (1271–1368) 5–6, 81, 141 n.45
Yue Meiti 岳美緹 of Shanghai 127 n.96
yueju 越劇 70, 73, 102, 127 n.95

zaju 雜劇 80, 90, 116 n.4, 136 n.12
Zang Maoxun 臧懋循 140 n.44
Zeng Jingping 曾静萍 34, 38–9, 42, 55–6, 72–3, 85, 89–90, 94, 99, 125 n.81
Zhang Aiding 張艾丁 31–2
Zhang, Everett 142 n.55
Zhang Jingjing 張婧婧 103–6
The Imperial Stele Pavilion 46, 57, 71, 92, 102–6
Li Shishi 李師師 106

Zhangzhou 7–8, 16, 21, 84, 112 n.16
Zhao Zhennü 趙真女 82, 137 n.18
Zhejiang 14, 22, 73, 92
Zheng He 鄭和 6
Zheng Yuanhe 鄭元和 77, 82
Zhou Weizhi 周巍峙 32
Zhu Bian 朱弁 32, 71, 81
Zhu Maichen 90–5, 141 n.45, 141 n.48
Zhu Shouchang 朱壽昌 84
Zhu Wen and the Lucky Coins (*Zhu Wen Taiping qian* 朱文太平錢) 32, 53, 88–9
Zhu Wen Flees the Ghost (*Zhu Wen zou gui* 朱文走鬼) 89
Zhu Xi 朱熹 21
Zhuang Dingshui 莊鼎水 48–9
zuibaixi 嘴白戲 (talking scenes) 90, 141 n.46